Toddler Day Care

Toddler Day Care

A Guide to Responsive Caregiving

Robin Lynn Leavitt
Brenda Krause Eheart

Psychology Department and Institute for
    Child Behavior and Development
University of Illinois at Urbana–Champaign

Lexington Books
D.C. Heath and Company/Lexington, Massachusetts/Toronto

Library of Congress Cataloging in Publication Data

Leavitt, Robin Lynn.
    Toddler Day Care

    Bibliography: p.
    Includes index.
    1. Day care centers. 2. Children—Institutional care. 3. Child development.
4. Education, Preschool. I. Eheart, Brenda Krause. II. Title.
HV851.L43   1985   362.7′ 12′ 068   84-40741
ISBN 0-669-09980-5 (alk. paper)
ISBN 0-669-09981-3 (pbk.: alk. paper)

Published simultaneously in Canada
Printed in the United States of America on acid-free paper
International Standard Book Number: 0-669-09980-5 Casebound
International Standard Book Number: 0-669-09981-3 Paperbound
Library of Congress Catalog Card Number: 84-40741

To my mother and father who have known and demonstrated the meaning of responsive caregiving, and to my seven nieces and nephews whom I have loved through toddlerhood.

Robin Lynn Leavitt

To the memories of Leon Charles Krause, who showed me the meaning of responsive caregiving in his personal life, and Carol J. Porter, who enhanced our understanding of responsive caregiving in her professional life.

Brenda Krause Eheart

Contents

Foreword

Valerie Polakow (Suransky)

When I read this book I thought of many children that I have met in child-care centers over the years. I thought of children like four-year-old Seth who hates his "yukkie poo-poo school" because there's never time to play with blocks in the basement, children like five-year-old Sharon who's bright but whose teachers tell me "thinks the wrong way." I heard the voice of Bobby, sobbing in the corner of his franchise day-care center while his untrained, underpaid eighteen-year-old aide looked on. Fleeting images of shopping-mall day care appeared: images of plastic smells and textures; lethargic children in "drop-in" rooms, disconnected from the spirit of life; children whose creativity and vitality have been eroded by mindless care. As I think of these children, living out their lives in *anti-child* centers, I suddenly wish I could gather them up on a magic flying carpet and whisk them over to the Infant-Toddler Center at Urbana–Champaign, there to enjoy an infancy and early childhood where they are free to touch, to talk, to move, and to play.

This text, by Robin Leavitt and Brenda Krause Eheart, is a fine example of the integration of personal-practical knowledge gained from direct experience working with young children, and appropriate developmental research. The sensitive observations of toddlers described in this book, and the way these observations are used to develop another model of evaluation, are in the tradition of qualitative descriptive research, such as we find in the work of other exemplary educators like Patricia Carini and Michael Armstrong.

Teachers will find this text very valuable. It is clearly written, thoughtful, and sensitive to the complexities of the world of day care. I particularly appreciate the child-centered perspective taken by the authors. Their commitment to child-initiated (rather than adult-directed) play, to careful *child watching*, and to parent collaboration displays a much needed awareness of the direction child care in this country should take. Unfortunately, when we survey the deplorable disarray of daycare options available to working parents under the present administration, we find that centers such as ITC are still the exception rather than the rule.

Toddler Day Care: A Guide to Responsive Caregiving is a good and hopeful beginning, a catalyst for change in the arid landscape of burgeoning child-care-for-profit businesses and adult-centered bureaucratic preschools. This text describes how the early lives of children can be different, play-filled and mutually enriching for caregivers and toddlers. In such a child-friendly landscape we see a vision of other possibilities, of what child care in this country could become; for it is not the *erosion*, but rather the *celebration*, of childhood that we should foster. *Toddler Day Care* points the way.

Acknowledgments

This book would not have been possible without the participation of the children, parents, and staff of the University of Illinois Infant-Toddler Center (ITC). The children showed us how to enter their worlds, and helped us rediscover the magic of toddlerhood. Their parents helped us understand the concerns, frustrations, and joys involved in coordinating parenting and day care. The tireless flexibility and professional commitment of the ITC staff, especially Monica Avis, Nadine Grudzien, Jacalynn Hardesty, Dorothy Kohlberg, Meredith Lewis, Gloria Mathias, Clara Pinkham, and Sherry Smith, helped us understand the application of responsive caregiving in the day-to-day world of toddler day care.

For their encouragement and assistance, we also acknowledge our colleagues at the Institute for Child Behavior and Development, especially Dr. Robert L. Sprague, who saw us through many day-care operating crises, and Dr. Esther Sleator, our friend and pediatric consultant.

We are especially grateful to Joyce Wolverton who has spent countless hours at the word processor, patiently typing and retyping our manuscript, organizing references, and attending to the numerous details involved in preparing a final manuscript. She was invaluable.

Special appreciation also goes to all our editors at Lexington Books, and to Dorothy O'Connell of Champaign who edited our first draft.

To Wayland, Sarah, and Seth a special thank-you for their constant patience and love while living with a career wife and mother.

And, finally, for the hours he has spent listening to Robin clarify aloud her thoughts about toddler care and for his enduring love and support for her professional endeavors, Bill deserves a very special thanks.

Introduction

The need for meaningful and practical information about toddler caregiving is becoming critical. The number of toddlers being enrolled in day-care centers is increasing dramatically as more and more of their mothers join the work force. We are very concerned about the quality of care these toddlers receive as they enter day care. Our concern stems from the trend in this country to overvalue the importance of achievement and accomplishment for young children, and to undervalue the importance of training for caregivers in day care. We are disheartened by the impact of these trends on toddler day-care programs. For example, instead of stressing the importance of a developmental, child-centered approach to caregiving, many programs seem to be teacher-dominated, with a focus on early academics and arbitrary routines. These programs can prevent toddlers from experiencing a happy childhood and may short-change their physical, emotional, social, and creative growth.

We believe that childhood is an important period for its own sake, and that caregivers must learn to be responsive, rather than directive. Responsive caregiving requires first the integration and application of knowledge from several disciplines, including psychology, sociology, medicine, and education. Second, responsive caregiving stresses the importance of entering the toddler's world in day care, rather than imposing our world on her.[1] Consequently, for us the term "caregiver" refers to a *child development specialist—* someone who is able to apply extensive knowledge of child development to the day-to-day world of group care in order to foster the development of the total child.

For the past six years, through the Developmental Child Care Program, University of Illinois at Urbana-Champaign, we have directed the Infant-Toddler Center (the ITC) and trained students to provide quality day care for infants and toddlers.

We focused our efforts primarily on learning what caregivers need to know in order to provide quality care. Specifically, we were committed to learning how to apply research and theory to day-care settings in order to provide infants and toddlers with a safe and healthy environment that fostered their development. We paid careful attention to developing a daily program that provided each child with a happy infancy or toddlerhood—a time when children could be themselves and find themselves.[2]

The need to help day-care workers become responsive child development specialists, and the need for practical information about toddler caregiving, prompted us to begin writing and organizing what we had learned through our experience at the ITC in caring for over one hundred toddlers, and in teaching countless students. Our professional respect for caregivers, and our commitment to the well-being of young children and their families inspired us to share our findings with caregivers, students, faculty, and parents . . . with you.

We have written about toddlers, children between fifteen and thirty-six months of age, because we could find so little related to toddlers in group care to guide us. Textbooks were insufficient and there were few exemplary centers in our community. Our caregivers and students needed a comprehensive guide to toddler day care that focused on the distinct characteristics and needs of toddlers, and that illustrated how toddler day care is different from preschool or infant care.

In all that we have learned, two themes emerge as paramount. One is the extreme importance and intellectual challenge of applying child-development research and theory to group care for young children. The other is the importance of following the toddler's lead, as she invites us to understand and enhance her world. These two themes are the essence of responsive caregiving. The responsive caregiver's role in the daily world of group caregiving for toddlers is illustrated throughout this text. Chapter 1 discusses toddler development and its implications for program planning. Chapter 2 reviews the importance of play in a toddler's life, and shows how to support play in toddler day care. Chapters 3 and 4 examine how to plan physical environments for toddlers and how to manage routines throughout the day. Chapters 5 and 6 offer suggestions for guiding toddlers' behavior and assessing their development. Our concluding chapters focus on relationships with parents, on health and safety components of toddler day care, and finally, on the caregiver as a professional.

Throughout the book, we stress the need to create child-centered day-care environments that are based on the developmental and individual needs of toddlers. We also emphasize the joys and demands of providing quality care. We recognize that providing full day care for toddlers is an exhilarating, challenging, and sometimes exhausting occupation. It requires both knowledge and commitment. We bring to you our knowledge, which we hope will, in turn, strengthen your commitment.

Notes

1. To avoid the clumsy repetition of "he/she" throughout the text, we use "he" and "she" in alternating chapters. Hence, chapters 1, 3, 5, 7, and 9 refer to the toddler as "he," chapters 2, 4, 6, and 8 as "she."

2. This definition of a happy childhood is borrowed from Alison Clarke-Stewart, *Child care in the family: A review of research and some propositions for policy* (New York: Academic Press, 1977).

Toddler Day Care

1
The Development of Toddlers

There's nobody else in the world, and the world was made for me.
"The Island," A.A. Milne, 1924

Responsive caregiving for toddlers requires a recognition of children's developmental needs and interests. For day-care center staff, this recognition can be translated into a statement of goals, which then can serve as the basis for program development. Alison Clarke-Stewart (1977), in an extensive review of child-care research, proposes that a child-care program should have three major goals. The first goal is to provide for the physical survival of all children. This minimum requirement is of the highest priority. Clarke-Stewart next recommends that we try to offer children a "happy childhood—a time free from pressures and stress, a time for children to be themselves, find themselves, and express themselves" (p. 83). Clarke-Stewart's third goal is to promote "development of the whole child" (p. 84). Beginning with this chapter, this text explores how caregivers can best meet these three goals.

Consideration of all the above goals requires an understanding of all the factors influencing a child's development. Therefore, we begin with an examination of three main influences on toddler development: individual biological inheritance; evolutionary inheritance; and the family, community, and cultural environment. Individual biological inheritance refers to the characteristics the child inherits from his parents (Kaplan, 1973). The combination of these characteristics makes every child unique and different. Biological traits include physical appearance, temperament, sex, and color of hair, eyes, and skin. We gain knowledge of the child's individual biological heritage by observations of and interactions with each child.

Evolutionary inheritance refers to the inborn patterns of development and behavior that children of any age have in common with their same-age peers (Kaplan, 1973). Most toddlers, for example, are walking and beginning to develop self-awareness. By eighteen months of age, most children also have developed strong attachments to their primary caregivers—usually their parents. As we care for and observe toddlers, and as we learn more about theories of development, we acquire knowledge of toddler development.

Caregivers need to be aware of a third factor: the influence that the family, community, and cultural environment have on children and on the caregiver's own attitudes and behaviors towards children. (These three factors are discussed in more detail later in this chapter.)

Theoretical Perspectives on Development

Influences on child development have been documented by generations of researchers and theorists. These theorists often vary widely in their interpretations and explanations of children's developmental characteristics. This is a result of their different perspectives on the nature of human development, their tendency to focus on different areas of development, and the fact that research on children's development is far from complete.

Each theorist's perspective is usually based on a belief that development is influenced primarily by one's biology or one's environment. One perspective, that of maturationists such as Gesell, describes development as an internal, biological process: a child develops as his innate capabilities unfold (Gesell and Ilg, 1949; Mead, 1976; Stevens and King, 1976). At the opposite end of this continuum are behaviorists such as Skinner. Behaviorists see the child as a passive organism shaped by environmental stimuli, which can be manipulated to produce desired behavior (Mead, 1976; Skinner, 1953, 1974; Stevens and King, 1976). Between these two extremes lie the perspectives of interactionists such as Piaget and Erikson. These theorists see the individual's development as influenced by both heredity and interaction with the environment (Mead, 1976; Stevens and King, 1976).

In addition to maintaining different assumptions about the nature of development, theorists usually focus on one specific area of development. For example, although both are interactionists, Piaget focused on cognitive development while Erikson focused on emotional development. The combination of different assumptions and concentrations result in different characterizations of toddlerhood. For Piaget the dominant theme is the development of symbolic thinking (Ginsberg and Opper, 1969); Erikson emphasizes the toddler's growing autonomy (Mead, 1976); while Kagan concludes that toddler behaviors indicate the emergence of self-awareness (Kagan, 1981).

A review of leading developmental theories also reveals that over time, as research continues on child development, new theoretical perspectives emerge. Sometimes new findings contradict previously held beliefs. For example, Piaget saw the toddler as totally self-absorbed or egocentric. Very recently Kagan (1981) described the toddler's growing capacity for empathy and regard for others. For caregivers working directly with toddlers, their own experiences and observations will also change and continually influence their understanding of toddler development.

Because no one theorist can completely explain the development of the whole child, caregivers must draw upon all theories of development, as well as their own experiences. Caregivers then can integrate and apply this information as they continually formulate program goals and implement caregiving practices. To help you in this endeavor, the following sections review the three main influences on toddler development which are described in the child-development literature, and which significantly influence caregiving practices.

Individual Biological Inheritance

Our biological heritage makes each of us a unique human being. When we, as caregivers, are faced in toddler day care with five, ten, or even more children, it is essential that we come to know these children well (see chapter 6). As we become better acquainted with them, we recognize differences in each toddler's physical appearance—Johnny is very small for his age; Heidi stands out because of her flaming red hair and face full of freckles. We also recognize the important role of sex in each child's behavior, as girls and boys often display stereotypical behaviors.

Of all aspects of biological inheritance, a toddler's temperament may have the most important influence on the caregiver's attitudes and behavior toward him. Children vary in temperament. Some are more attentive than others, some more irritable. Some toddlers are easily comforted, some are not. Some toddlers seem to be active all of the time, others may be more passive.

In the past few years, research on children's temperamental differences has suggested that there are three distinct kinds of response patterns: the average child; the active child; and the quiet or slow-to-warm-up child (Brazelton, 1974; Chess and Thomas, 1973). The average child adapts easily to change, is usually in a good mood, can be comforted easily, and reacts to his social and physical environment in a moderate rather than passive or intensive way.

The active child is sometimes falsely labeled "hyperactive." This child seems to be on-the-go all the time, is sometimes accident prone, and, in general, seems to demand the caregiver's constant attention. He is also intense: he will eat with intensity, play with intensity, and observe you with intensity.

The antithesis of the active child is the quiet child. This toddler approaches his environment with caution and responds with passivity. He is silent, watchful, and slow-to-warm-up, rarely expressing either great joy or distress.

Observant caregivers usually are able to classify children's temperaments after only a few weeks. Then it is up to the caregiver to adjust to the temperamental qualities of each child. This may be a challenge, but like all challenges, it may end up being very rewarding for both toddler and caregiver. For example, the active child may exhaust the caregiver by day's end, simply because he demands constant supervision or attention in order to keep him safe. However, he also is an exciting child to watch, as he displays great curiosity and intense enjoyment while exploring his world and engaging caregivers in earnest conversation.

By getting to know and accept each toddler as a unique individual, caregivers can begin to provide programs that offer children a "happy childhood" in which children can be themselves and find themselves.

Evolutionary Inheritance

Just as each child inherits individual characteristics at birth, all children have in common an evolutionary inheritance. This refers to characteristics and behavior that children have in common with all other same-age peers. The growing competencies toddlers exhibit in motor skills, language, and cognition are intertwined and complex, and are strongly tied to emotional and social development, as toddlers grow in their understanding of themselves and their world. This section reviews the most salient developmental characteristics of toddlers. Caregivers need to consider each of the following characteristics in relation to the toddler's total development. For more in-depth information, we strongly recommend that caregivers refer to several books specifically concerned with toddler development (e.g., Brazelton, 1974; Kagan, 1981; White, 1975).

Awareness of His Own Competencies

Toddlers have made impressive advances in their large and fine motor abilities, and they become quite aware of what they can and cannot do (Kagan, 1981). Most fifteen-month-olds are walking, perhaps awkwardly, but unassisted. By three years they are running full tilt, laughing and confident. Toddlers show great pride in their accomplishments. They know when they have successfully completed a task or mastered a skill. They smile and happily exclaim "Me do it!" or "All done!" At the same time, they become aware of their limitations. They show considerable distress when asked to do tasks they feel unable to master.

Awareness of Standards

Kagan (1981) describes how toddlers exhibit concern over events and behavior they have learned violate adult standards. They are developing an appreciation of right and wrong in regard to physical objects as well as behavior.

They want these standards to be maintained and are aroused by their violation. Upon discovering a broken toy or untied shoelace, toddlers may exclaim "Oh-oh," and will seek out someone to put things right again. They regard these events quite seriously. We have noticed toddlers getting quite upset when the room has been rearranged and things do not belong in familiar places.

Complex Understanding and Use of Language

The toddler makes enormous advances in his comprehension and use of language. He understands words, questions, and comments, and can follow simple directions. His vocabulary grows, with little explicit instruction, from about 19 words at fifteen months, to 270 words by two years, then jumping to about 950 by three years of age (Mussen, P., Conger, J. and Kagan, J., 1964; Sutton-Smith, 1973). Furthermore, he understands that words have meaning, as he labels objects ("doggie," "chair"). He continually seeks out the names of new and familiar objects, repeatedly pointing to them and bringing them to adults to label.

The toddler begins to combine words to describe events in his immediate environment ("fall down"). He becomes preoccupied with his own actions and constantly describes them ("I go out," "I drink juice"). In addition, the toddler learns to communicate his desires, expecting adults to respond to his demands ("More milk"). Toddlers enjoy their new communication skills and eagerly engage others in conversation.

Egocentrism vs. Empathy

The toddler is primarily concerned with himself and his immediate world. He now recognizes himself, reflected in the mirror and in photographs. When a caregiver plays the game "Who is that?" with a toddler, pointing to his image, he gleefully responds "Me!" His interest in himself is apparent in his delight in describing his own actions or in hearing a caregiver describe them.

The toddler's egocentric perspective is also apparent in his belief that because *he* is alive and has feelings, all else in the world is alive and conscious (Pulaski, 1978). Brenda's daughter, at age two, was afraid at dusk. She would run to her mother and say, "The dark coming, it's going to get me!" Often at the ITC, we hear children exclaiming, "Ball hurt me!" or "Bad chair!" as they accidentally trip and fall.

This egocentrism also means that the young toddler sees things from his own point of view. He does not see the consequences of his own actions towards others. For example, it's difficult to convince a toddler that when he hits another child he is hurting the child. A capacity for empathy does emerge during toddlerhood, however, as children gradually become capable of recognizing how others feel. They hug a child who hurts himself, and may give a toy to a crying child to comfort him. Gradually, with the help of responsive caregivers, this empathic capacity leads the older toddler to understand the consequences of his own aggressive behavior.

Emergence of Symbolic Thinking

As he interacts with his environment, the toddler learns about his immediate world. In this process he depends on real objects and experiences. He must still use his senses to examine and explore materials and to discover the relationships among objects. Suransky (1982) describes a day-care scene where children are shown a picture of a feather, and upon being told to do so, are expected to associate it with the adjective "light." However, we know toddlers cannot learn this concept from a picture; they need to see, touch, and hold a *real* feather while adults help them to label and describe what they see and feel.

As the toddler grows, however, he tends to experiment less and less on the external, physical level, and more often on the internal, mental level. This indicates his emerging capacity for symbolic thinking, or the ability to use mental symbols or words to represent absent objects and past events (Ginsberg and Opper, 1969). In other words, the toddler begins to visualize what will succeed and what will fail, relying less on physical trial and error (Pulaski, 1978). For example, we've observed toddlers examining puzzle pieces and deliberately fitting them in place, one by one, making no mistakes. This new capacity is also demonstrated by toddlers in dramatic and imaginative play, as they evoke past experiences by imitating absent adults. For example, a toddler may imitate his parent preparing supper or talking on the telephone. This new ability is tied closely to the toddler's rapidly increasing comprehension and use of words, as just described. Parents and caregivers describe children who are able to represent actions mentally, instead of acting them out, as more thoughtful and much less impulsive than children who must try possible solutions in the open rather than in their heads. For all caregivers, this emergence of symbolic thinking ability is a remarkable phenomenon.

Independence vs. Dependence

The toddler's growing intellectual and physical competence often conflicts with his emotional security. It often seems the more independent he appears, the more dependent he becomes. The child, feeling his physical strength and struggling to establish his own identity, often resists adult controls. He insists on doing for himself and determining his own actions. Caregivers who attempt to do for the toddler (in their hurry to put away a puzzle or dress children for play) are admonished "No! Me do it!" The toddler must pull out his hair at lunch and put his hat in his cubby himself.

The toddler, however, also seems to realize that he is a very small child in big world. He needs special adults in his life to keep him safe. A toddler in a day-care center may follow a favorite caregiver around, wanting to and play. Or he may dart away, as he practices his new-found mobility, expect the caregiver to run after him to make sure he is safe. He may climb to the top of a slide and then be afraid to come down.

Conclusion

Observing, listening to, and interacting with toddlers, as they explore and describe their ever-expanding world, is fascinating, no matter how many times a caregiver witnesses it. Part of this fascination derives from their amazing rate of growth and discovery, as well as the contradictions in their behavior. Perhaps there is no greater challenge to caregivers than keeping up with the day-to-day changes and contradictions in development which a group of toddlers presents.

Family, Community, and Cultural Influences

So far, we have discussed how toddlers develop as unique individuals because of their individual biological inheritance. We also have examined how they develop as a group because of their evolutionary inheritance. In order to understand toddler development more fully, we must also examine how these factors interact with the toddler's environment, which is comprised of his family, his community, and his culture (Bronfenbrenner, 1974). A toddler's parents strongly influence his development. That influence is dependent on parent characteristics including their ages, temperaments, knowledge of child development, and child-rearing beliefs. Development also is influenced as a child interacts with other family members. It may be important for caregivers to know, for example, whether a toddler is an only child, the second child, or perhaps the only boy in a family with four girls.

Belsky (1980) points out that, in addition to appreciating the influence of the immediate family unit, we must also understand "the embeddedness of the individual and the family within larger social units" (p. 327). For example, there are factors that exert influence on the family such as the world of work and the neighborhood. These factors are strongly tied to a family's socioeconomic status, which, in turn, has been found to influence the behavior of parents, family size and structure, and the physical environment of the home (Clarke-Stewart, 1977).

In addition to the family's socioeconomic status, the child-rearing beliefs of the day-care staff strongly influence the care provided, which, in turn, influences the development of the children in their charge. Carol Porter (1980) suggests that day-care teachers' theoretical beliefs, which serve as a rationale for program practices, are based on their early relationships and experiences. In Porter's study, advanced education was viewed by day-care personnel as an experience that confirmed rather than challenged their existing methods and rationales.

Beliefs about how to provide proper care for children stem not only from early experiences, but also from each culture's strongest suppositions about the essence of human nature. Jerome Kagan (1982) describes Japanese parents' strong beliefs about child development, which differ from North American parents' views. These beliefs influence parental actions. Kagan writes:

> Japanese mothers believe infants do not have a special tendency to develop a deeply dependent relationship with them. Because a profound interdependence between parent and child is valued in Japanese culture, Japanese mothers rush to soothe their babies whenever they cry and sleep with them at night, often until they are five or six years old (p. 474).

North Americans, by contrast, believe young children are basically dependent. Kagan writes that American mothers want their children to be autonomous, but are afraid their infants will remain dependent. "Hence, American mothers try to encourage self-reliance by typically waiting a while before going to care for their crying infant, especially if it is a boy" (p. 474).

Another example of cultural influence on the caregiver's behavior is the societal attitude toward violence and corporal punishment (Alvy, 1975). Physical punishment, as a means of controlling children's behavior, is practiced with extraordinary frequency in this country (Gelles, 1978; Strauss, 1971). It is also condoned by many would-be sources of influence on caregiving behavior. Viano (as reported in Belsky, 1980) reports that, of those questioned, two out of every three educators, police officers, and clerics condoned spanking with the hand. No wonder parents and day-care providers often view spanking as one of (perhaps) many means of controlling children's behavior.

The above examples are only two of many cultural influences on caregiver behaviors. Of all the influences on caregiver behaviors and hence on children's development, we are probably least aware of cultural suppositions. Most adults are much more aware of how their families and communities influence them than of the influence of the culture. It is important, then, that caregivers try to analyze the basis for their behaviors toward children. In doing so, they will be better able to evaluate their caregiving skills. Only after we recognize how our families, communities, and cultural practices influence us, can be begin to evaluate our attitudes and beliefs, and ultimately, our behaviors, which so profoundly influence the development of the children in our care.

Summary

We cannot take seriously enough the commitment to provide quality care to young children in day-care programs. This care, we have suggested, stems from program goals which are based on the caregiver's understanding of children's evolutionary and individual biological heritage, and on an appreciation of how the children and their families respond to their social and cultural environment.

In the remaining chapters, we examine how knowledge of the individual toddler, of toddler development, and of the toddler's family, community, and cultural environment may be applied to create day-care programs that promote safe, healthy, happy children, and promote the development of the whole child.

References

Alvy, K. 1975. Preventing child abuse. *American Psychologist* 30, 921–928.

Belsky, J. 1980. Child maltreatment: An ecological integration. *American Psychologist* 35, 320–335.

Brazelton, T. 1974. *Toddlers and parents.* New York: Delacorte Press.

Bronfenbrenner, U. 1974. *The ecology of human development.* Cambridge, MA: Harvard University Press.

Chess, S., and Thomas, A. 1973. Temperament in the normal infant. In J. Westman (ed.), *Individual differences in children.* New York: John Wiley & Sons.

Clarke-Stewart, A. 1977. *Child care in the family: A review of research and some propositions for policy.* New York: Academic Press.

Gelles, R. 1978. Violence towards children in the United States. *American Journal of Orthopsychiatry* 48, 580–592.

Gesell, H., and Ilg, F.L. 1949. *Child development: An introduction to the study of human growth.* New York: Harper and Row.

Ginsberg, H., and Opper, S. 1969. *Piaget's theory of intellectual development: An introduction.* Englewood Cliffs, NJ: Prentice-Hall.

Kagan, J. 1981. *The second year—the emergence of self-awareness.* Cambridge, MA: Harvard University Press.

Kagan, J. 1982. Canalization of early psychological development. *Pediatrics* 70, 474–483.

Kaplan, L. 1973. *Oneness and separateness: From infant to individual.* New York: Bantam.

Mead, D.E. 1976. *Six approaches to child rearing.* Provo, UT: Brigham Young University Press.

Milne, A.A. 1952. The Island. In *When we were very young.* New York: E.P. Dutton (Originally published 1924).

Mussen, P.; Conger, J.; and Kagan, J. 1964. *Child development and personality.* New York: Harper & Row.

Porter, C. 1980. *Voices from the preschool: Perspectives of early childhood educators.* Unpublished doctoral dissertation, State University of New York at Buffalo.

Pulaski, M. 1978. *Your baby's mind and how it grows: Piaget's theory for parents.* New York: Harper & Row.

Skinner, B.F. 1953. *Science and human behavior.* New York: Free Press.

Skinner, B.F. 1974. *About behaviorism.* New York: Knopf.

Stevens, J., and King, E. 1976. *Administering early childhood education programs.* Boston: Little, Brown & Co.

Strauss, M. 1971. Some social antecedents of physical punishment: A linkage theory interpretation. *Journal of Marriage and the Family* 33, 658–663.

Suransky, V. 1982. *The erosion of childhood.* Chicago: University of Chicago Press.

Sutton-Smith, B. 1973. *Child psychology.* Englewood Cliffs, NJ: Prentice-Hall.

White, B. 1975. *The first three years of life.* Englewood Cliffs, NJ: Prentice-Hall.

2
Toddlers' Play

Play is not only the child's response to life; it is his life if he is to be a
vital, growing, creative individual.

Hartley and Goldenson, 1963

hapter 1 described the development of toddlers. In this chapter, we
explore the central role of play in fostering this development. First,
we examine the importance of play in a toddler's life. Next, we describe how toddlers play and how caregivers can support and plan for play in
a child-centered, developmental day-care program. We end the chapter with
a brief discussion of the importance of child-directed play in toddler day care.

The Importance of Play for Toddlers

When we observe toddlers at play, we often see their enjoyment and delight.
We may note how intensely a child is absorbed and how she concentrates.
What may not be clear to us is how important this play is for the child's development. Researchers suggest that children learn and develop through complex learning experiences which may appear to be trivial and just "child's
play" from an adult perspective (Strother, 1982).

Too often, adults assume that play is a form of diversion or amusement,
not to be taken seriously. But for toddlers, play is an important activity, for it
is the way they learn about themselves and their world. *It is the central activity of childhood.* Through play experiences, children begin to master many
fundamental physical, social, and intellectual skills and concepts (Isenberg
and Jacobs, 1982). This has been well documented in the research literature.
For example, see Elder and Pederson (1978), Fein (1981), and Ungerer, Zelazo, Kearsley, and O'Leary (1981) for research on play and cognitive development; and Bruner, Jolly, and Sylva (1976), Garvey (1977), Guralnich
(1981), and Vandenberg (1981) for research on play and social development.

Cretney (1972) has fully described how play influences a toddler's total
development. She writes:

Table 2–1
Partial List of Developmental Skills

Language	Gross Motor	Fine Motor	Cognitive	Emotional	Social
listening	balancing	scribbling	matching	liking self	participating
responding	rolling	stacking	classifying	expressing feelings	sharing
interpreting	dancing	zipping	creating	seeking comfort	awareness of others' feelings
singing	pushing & pulling	folding	discriminating	working alone	seeking attention
describing	climbing	grasping	attending	expressing pride	expressing empathy
requesting	tossing	pouring	representing actions mentally	understanding feelings	learning acceptable and unacceptable behavior
questioning	running	turning pages	following directions	adjusting to changes	helping
labeling	jumping	stirring	remembering	receiving affection	pretending
conversing	kicking	pounding	understanding cause and effect	asserting independence	following and leading peers
		scooping	awareness of competencies		

Through play he strengthens his muscles, develops his coordination and his senses . . . and learns new skills. Play can stimulate creativity and the use of his imagination; it enables him to try out various solutions as he tackles a problem; it gives him the opportunity to practice everyday tasks of life; it provides a means to expend excess energy and for the release of tension; it helps him learn how to get along with people, both individually and in groups; it gives him an awareness of the values and symbols of his world (pp. 5–6).

Cretney has described how toddlers, through play, learn about the present; they also develop skills for future learning. Table 2–1 lists some of the skills that are enhanced through play in each of the major developmental areas.

How Toddlers Play

As we recognize the importance of play in the lives of toddlers, it is also important to understand *how* they play in order to enhance their play in the day-care environment. As child-care professionals, we understand how significant play is for children's development; but for the toddlers, play is an end in itself. Toddlers have no need for final products or even for completing a task (Stone and Church, 1973; Suransky, 1982). For them, products are subordinate to the *process* of playing. And for toddlers given freedom of time and space, play usually involves choosing and pursuing activities on their own. These activities are primarily characterized by active exploration of what they can do with their bodies and with materials and equipment. In choosing their own activities, toddlers are acting on their environment and learning through their own actions. They cannot process information secondhand as adults or older children do, so they ". . . need to construct their understanding bit by bit by experiencing their environment, testing their new skills and building confidence to undertake more difficult activities" (Fewell and Vadasy, 1983, p. 4).

Toddlers who are given the freedom to be self-directed in their play master not only intellectual skills, but physical, social, language, and emotional skills as well. For example, a two-year-old who makes a simple construction out of blocks and who seeks and receives approval for her accomplishment, is experimenting and developing fine motor, social, language, and intellectual skills. She is also demonstrating pride in a personal accomplishment, an accomplishment that she initiated. The ability to demonstrate pride in the development of a new skill or in a creation of one's own is a foundation block for later competence (White, 1975). For caregivers, there are few rewards as exciting and joyful as participating in a toddler's demonstration of pride in a personal accomplishment.

The above example demonstrates how toddlers' play can encompass several developmental areas. For purposes of clarification, however, the following discussion separates toddlers' play into separate developmental categories.

Fine and Gross Motor Development

The active play of toddlers involves many gross and fine motor activities. Toddlers love to run, although some are still awkward; they like to jump and bounce, to swing, to climb up, in, and out. They maneuver around the play yard on small riding toys and like to push and pull carts, wagons, and other toys on wheels (even those with no wheels!).

Although large-muscle activity is usually preferred to small-muscle activity, the toddler enjoys exploring any toys or objects at hand "such as pots, pans, and kitchen utensils; he fingers, pokes, and pulls; he assembles, sorts, and builds; he imitates common uses of objects and creates uses of his own" (Fowler, 1980, p. 142). While these activities help to develop small-muscle coordination, they also play a role in the toddler's cognitive development.

Cognitive Development

The development of intelligence for toddlers involves their ability to control impulses and emotions; to expand imaginative role play; and to produce creations, such as scribbled drawings or towers of blocks (White, 1975). Toddlers enjoy gathering materials, filling and dumping containers of objects, carrying them about; they like to hammer and pound, stack and knock down blocks. Clearly, they are beginning to learn cause and effect. Toddlers also take pleasure in the trial-and-error manipulation involved in puzzles, connecting blocks, and large pegboards.

Sensory play for toddlers includes scooping and pouring sand, water, cornmeal, or beans. A favorite activity at the ITC is filling a small plastic swimming pool with styrofoam packing material for the toddlers to feel and experiment with. While many toddlers are sensitive about keeping their hands clean, they enjoy rolling and shaping playdough, wet sand, or mud, and they enjoy fingerpainting. Toddlers' experiences in painting vary widely depending on whether they use an easel or a table; use large or small brushes; or work with watercolors or tempera. This manipulative and sensory play provides toddlers with opportunities to classify, construct, and reconstruct (Harness, 1979).

Social and Emotional Development

Sometimes a toddler's play is quiet; she prefers to just watch and listen. ITC staff often have observed a toddler in a corner, alone, happily turning the pages of a picture book. At other times, the toddler may prefer to curl up on a couch with her blanket and stuffed animal and watch the others.

Young toddlers typically play alone, even though they may be curious about others, and are sometimes resentful of other children's intrusions on their play. They often play near or alongside other children, but initially there is little interaction, except perhaps to dispute over a toy. However, we notice that eventually many toddlers begin to attempt to communicate with their peers, moving close to kiss or pat another. This often turns into a bite or hit, as the youngest children do not yet understand how others feel, or realize the impact of their behavior on others (see chapter 1). This kind of interaction is often as experimental as their other kinds of play—the toddler usually does not intend to hurt. While ITC toddlers do not always play together, they intently observe each other. They often know whose clothes belong to whom (when the adults forget) and notify specific individuals when their parents come to pick them up.

As toddlers grow older and spend more time with each other, they play cooperatively, and even form deep friendships. Patrick shares a toy only with Tony. Meghann and Kerry often confer intimately while playing in the housekeeping area.

Toddlers also like to dress up and play house, boys and girls both setting tables and cooking, rocking dolls, and talking on the telephone. This dramatic play fosters the use of imagination, helps children to develop a sense of identity, and encourages cooperative play.

Toddlers like to have adults near them, not necessarily for interchange, but for company, comfort, and security (Stone and Church, 1973). They look to their caregivers for protection and assistance throughout the day.

They also like tickling, teasing, and playing pretend games. They take great delight in receiving special attention from their caregivers, often selecting one in particular to shadow.

Language Development

While toddlers are often found playing quietly by themselves, they can also be heard talking or singing to themselves as they play, sometimes babbling or repeating what they've heard adults or other children say earlier. Talking to Mom on the telephone is a favorite activity. Toddlers involve language (although it is limited for the youngest toddlers) in all aspects of their play, whether outdoors on the swing, inside with manipulatives, or listening to stories. Through play, they are learning to label their experiences and feelings, as well as to express them. Toddlers also increase their receptive vocabulary while playing with other children, interacting with adults, or quietly listening to a story or record.

Supporting Toddlers' Play

When the importance of play for toddlers is understood, as well as how they play, caregivers can begin to focus on supporting toddlers' play, so that the experience is meaningful, child-centered, and developmentally based. Three interactive components influence toddlers' play. These are the physical space, the individual child, and the role of the caregiver.

First, caregivers can enhance play by structuring a physical environment that encourages child-initiated and directed activities appropriate to the toddlers' development and interests. As toddlers learn primarily by interacting with their environment, a good setting for toddlers is one that invites them to explore and manipulate materials, with opportunities for making choices, for being challenged, and for succeeding. In such an environment, the children are free to act creatively, facilitated by the background efforts of the caregivers. The child is the doer—the caregiver the organizer (Fowler, 1980). A detailed discussion of the importance of physical space in toddler day care is presented in chapter 3.

A second component to consider is the individual child. Each child is unique with individual needs. The slow-to-warm-up child may need an unpressured, supportive atmosphere for play while the active child may need latitude (Clarke-Stewart, 1982).

The role of the caregiver is also extremely important. This role extends beyond arranging the environment, routine care (see chapter 4), and intervention in conflicts (see chapter 5). The caregiver, above all else, functions as a responsive participant in play. A description of this role follows.

Responsive Caregiving

Simply having things to look at, listen to, or play with is not enough to foster a toddler's development. It is also important that the child experience a responsive environment. Interactions between caregivers and toddlers determine, to a great extent, whether or not a responsive environment has been created.

A responsive caregiver is one who knows how to respond to a toddler's initiatives in play, expanding the scope of this play, while still allowing the toddler to take the lead. The adult tailors his or her behavior specifically to what the toddler is doing, and responds thoughtfully and appropriately. The caregiver carefully observes each child, alert for opportunities to elaborate on her play by suggesting new ideas or alternative toys and offering appropriate help or comments. In this way, the adult helps the child move ahead in all areas of development. The capacity for responsive caregiving grows with experience. However, new caregivers may also demonstrate such skills. To be responsive, caregivers must have an understanding of child development or the child's evolutionary inheritance. They must get to know each toddler as an individual with her own biological inheritance; and they must be interested in and appreciative of each child's family, community, and cultural environment. Caregivers also must be interested in and enthusiastic about the toddler's immediate world where so much is new, complicated, and intriguing, demanding exploration and information.

Responsive caregivers allow their personalities and particular strengths to surface when interacting with children. They are patient and flexible. Their conversation and comments are not artificial "teacher talk" ("What color are the peas?"), but are natural and unforced, arising out of the context of the play situation and dependent on the toddler's interests, skills, and needs.

Responsive caregivers avoid imposing their own ideas on the toddler, and attempt to see events from the child's perspective. They are supportive of the toddler's play, encouraging her in the way she uses materials. But they are also willing to withdraw from active participation in the toddler's play, knowing when and when not to intervene.

The following guidelines offer some suggestions for supporting play in a responsive environment.

Guidelines for Supporting Play

1. Observe children's play. Assess the children's general development and learn about the uniqueness of each child—her likes, dislikes, etc. You may find one child prefers block play consistently or that another seldom involves herself in dramatic play.
2. Take advantage of opportune moments for expanding the children's play. You can help them elaborate on their play by suggesting new ideas or adding new props to their play areas. Try to pick up on what a child says or does by asking open-ended questions, commenting, and describing what the child is doing. For example, plastic knives and miniature pastry rollers can be added to a playdough activity. Comments such as "Shannon, I see you're making your dough flat and thin. What will happen when you try to pick it up all at once?" give toddlers words for their actions and encourage them to experiment, and to reflect on their play.
3. Once a child is playing independently, avoid hovering, smothering her with attention. Encourage toddlers to explore and experiment with materials in their own ways. Use minimum direction. In the above example, the caregiver offered some props and some comments, but did not tell the children what to do, such as to roll their dough into balls or to make a pie.
4. Allow children to be as independent as they are able, and to do as much as they can for themselves. You might be tempted to show a child which way a puzzle piece goes, but encouraging her to try different angles until

she discovers the fit herself will result in a great feeling of accomplishment and encourage her involvement in new, challenging activities.

5. Avoid interrupting children's play, unless absolutely necessary for a scheduled routine such as lunch or a nap. (Remember to alert the children before scheduled routines.) Never interrupt child-directed play for an adult-directed activity.

6. Let toddlers know you are interested in what they do by encouraging them to talk about their play. For younger toddlers with limited language, review their play aloud. "Kimberly's poked her dough with lots of holes! Ryan's rolled his into one big ball!" They love to hear about themselves, and your interest will thrill them!

7. Assist children when they need it. (At least one caregiver in a team caregiving situation needs to maintain an awareness of the entire group, so children's needs can be met immediately.)

8. Avoid needless conversation with other caregivers. Be involved with children during play, even when stepping back to observe—see #1.

Planning for Play

Preparing the physical environment is the first step in planning for play, as we stated previously and discuss further in chapter 3. Opportunities for spontaneous exploration or play are provided by arranging a variety of materials so that they are accessible to the children. The toddlers should have long periods during the day to become involved freely and safely in self-directed play. During this play period, everyone is not doing the same thing at the same time. Some children may choose to play in the housekeeping area, others with puzzles, and still others with blocks. Providing this freedom for children does not mean that the children are totally in control. Nor does it imply that caregivers are "babysitting," that is, simply protecting children from harm. Caregivers are very active during toddler play periods. They follow the guidelines previously outlined. They employ all they know about toddler development and about each toddler as an individual. They encourage children to explore and experiment, to share, and to play within defined limits, and they help children learn about themselves and others.

Given the above, planning for play involves constantly reevaluating the materials available in relation to how they are used by the children, and consciously adding, rearranging, or changing the materials. In addition, caregivers plan for play by designing special experiences for the toddlers that they cannot initiate on their own. These are activities that the adult introduces, but the child's focus is still self-directed. These activities are introduced during the play period at opportune moments. *Children may or may not participate as they wish.*

These adult-initiated activities are based on the caregivers' daily observations of the children, as well as on formal assessments (see chapter 6). They also must meet the following criteria.

1. The activity *takes into account how toddlers come to know* or understand concepts and relationships (Spodek 1977). This allows children to learn through active experience and exploration. (The caregiver considers whether the child can use more than one sense to examine materials, can manipulate them over time, and whether they are real and familiar.)
2. The activity is *developmentally appropriate* (Spodek, 1977). It takes into account what toddlers know and can do while still exercising and challenging their emerging capabilities.
3. The experience is *worthwhile* (Spodek, 1977). In other words, through the experience the child will use or gain skills (see table 2–1) that will transfer for later learning. The activity is not something simply to keep her busy or produce an end product.

Some examples of play activities appropriate for toddlers are fingerpainting, dancing to records, lotto card games, water-table play, and stringing large beads. These activities need closer adult supervision for manageability and safety. They also are enhanced for the toddler through adult participation. Sally Goldberg has listed by developmental areas numerous program activities for toddlers. (See appendix A.)

Caregivers plan these activities in advance, except perhaps for the very experienced, who have learned to initiate activities spontaneously, drawing from the wealth of ideas they have accumulated over time. At the ITC, the toddler staff meets weekly to discuss the experiences they would like to provide for the toddlers, based on their observations and assessments. A weekly plan, summarizing the activities in one or two words, is posted and looks something like this:

Day	AM	PM
Monday	Fingerpainting Styrofoam pool	Water play Planting seeds
Tuesday	Playdough Pegboards	Easel painting Lotto cards
Wednesday	Cornmeal & beans Walk to flower garden	Dancing to records with scarves Crayon coloring

Thursday	Water play	Stringing beads
	Making pretzels	Watercolor painting
Friday	Musical instruments	Pasting tissue
	Chalk drawing on sidewalk	Obstacle course

A record of these plans is kept on file for review, so caregivers can be sure they are providing opportunities for a variety of experiences.

Introducing Planned Activities

In spite of the reams of knowledge we have amassed that show young children learn best through play, many caregivers set aside a special time during the day for a learning period or lesson time. During this time, adult-planned and adult-directed activities are introduced; all of the children must stop playing and participate. These activities usually are structured and formal; the caregiver has specific learning objectives in mind, which often result in a completed product to show that the toddlers have learned content information. The learning process then becomes secondary to this end product.

While the intent of these caregivers is often to foster development, the method is inappropriate for the toddler. The following vignette illustrates what too frequently happens just before and during a typical "activity" or "lesson time."

> The children are playing with various materials of their choice. At a predetermined time, the caregiver announces it is time to clean up. Amy must put her unfinished puzzle away. Another caregiver takes away Brian's and Ahmad's playdough. Block towers are tumbled and put away. Dress-up clothes are taken off and hung up. All the children's self-chosen activities are halted. All the children sit down on the rug around the teacher. She introduces the day's lesson by describing the theme for the month: weather. She holds up picture cards of rain, snow, wind, sun, and so on, labeling them and then quizzing the children about them. To emphasize the points made, the teacher tells the group to move to the art tables to color teacher-made outlines of the sun with yellow crayons. The children must color one, and only one sun, before they can return to free play. The next day, they will color clouds, and so on, until the unit is finished.

Several problems emerge in the lesson time described above. First, the children are not allowed to complete the activities in which they are already engaged. The children's self-chosen play is considered subordinate to the adult-planned activity. Thus, the teacher does not attempt to follow the children's lead in play, a critical part of responsive caregiving. The unspoken message the toddlers receive is that the teacher does not really value their play.

Second, the activity does not take into account how toddlers learn. The teacher expects the children to be passive recipients of information. Little is learned by quietly listening to an adult, and what is learned is not likely to be internalized, and is soon forgotten (Watrin and Furfey, 1978). A toddler's learning depends on the freedom to actively experience her environment. In addition, the teacher fails to account for individual differences in the capabilities and interests of the children. They are all expected to learn the same thing, the same way, at the same time.

Given that the caregiver in this example feels it is worthwhile for the children to begin to label and understand their experiences with different kinds of weather, a more appropriate approach would be to take advantage of incidental learning opportunities. For example, she could comment on the qualities of rain and snow *when they actually occur,* rather than creating an artificial situation and abstract representations. Toddlers play in the snow; scoop it and roll in it; feel how cold it is; see how it melts. By actively experiencing snow (or rain, or sunshine), with responsive caregivers to comment, label, describe, and answer their questions, toddlers are much more likely to internalize the information. And, in the process, they will develop skills for future learning.

We, the authors, cannot emphasize enough the importance and value of child-directed play and its particular appropriateness and role in a toddler day-care program. At the ITC child-directed play *is the curriculum,* regardless of whether the play is initiated by a child or an adult. Consequently, the daily schedule does not include specific times for "free play" and for "lessons," or "teacher-planned activities," or formal instruction. The caregiver's primary responsibility is to support child-directed play. How, then, do caregivers implement their planned activities?

Implementing the Adult-Initiated or Planned Activity

Caregivers are prepared to initiate most adult-planned activities at opportune moments. This means that there are no set times in which the activities must be done. For some activities, such as fingerpainting, water play or playdough, materials are prepared in early morning or during naptime. These activities are inviting play choices when the children arrive or awaken. An adult remains in the area to play with those children who choose to participate, while other toddlers become involved in different play activities that they choose. Some days, the posted activities are not introduced, because adults follow the children's lead in play when determining when and how to implement their planned activities.

The following example illustrates how an adult-initiated activity may be introduced:

The children were involved in play of their choice. Neil pushed a wheel toy, a few toddlers did puzzles in the manipulative area, Michael and Andy looked at books by themselves, two other children helped a caregiver fold the morning's laundry. Celia quietly wandered about watching the others.

Gary began to throw the farm animals he was playing with across the room and was redirected by the caregiver. Some minutes later he pushed Celia. The floating caregiver concluded that Gary might be bored, and that wandering Celia might be unable to make a play choice this morning. The caregiver invited both children to help her set up a crafts activity (the posted activity for the morning) in the art area. They helped her put out paste and paper, and sat at the table with her to make tissue collages.

Michael and Andy, finished with their books, noticed Gary and Celia's involvement and joined them. The other toddlers continued to play in interest areas of their choosing. Gary left the table to play outside, and Carin came in to try the pasting. And so it went; not all the children chose to participate, but those who did, did so at different times.

No child's play was interrupted to make her participate in the pasting activity—children came to and left the activity as they wished. The paste and paper remained available most of the morning, as some toddlers returned a second time. When the children lost interest, the caregiver asked two children to help put the materials away and wash the table. The two children then "helped" and watched the caregiver display all the children's creative collages on the classroom walls. Soon their parents would come and admire their artwork.

Sometimes, when a toddler cannot select from the play activities available, and resists adult suggestions, a caregiver can ask the child what she would like to do. Often this means the caregiver has to be flexible and take out pegboards, lotto cards, and musical instruments, when she hadn't planned on providing those specific choices for the children. This encourages the children to make independent choices. It gives them some control over their environment, and lets them know their choices are important. In addition, children will be more involved in play of their own choosing.

The following guidelines will help caregivers implement their planned activities.

Guidelines for Implementing Planned Activities

1. Plan small group activities for no more than three or four toddlers at a time. (This helps caregivers to individualize. Children spend less time waiting and more time doing. Interaction is also encouraged in small group activities.)
2. Allow children to do for themselves as much as possible. Avoid the impulse to make the activity easier for yourself by doing it for the children.

(We have frequently observed caregivers doing almost all the cutting and pasting in crafts activities. When this happens, the value of the experience for the children is lost.)

3. Do not expect too much or too little from the children. Try to prevent frustration and boredom. Expect toddlers to be messy, active, and protective of their toys and their space. At the same time, they can solve many of their own problems, can work on a project or activity of their own choosing for amazingly long periods, and can be responsible for returning materials to their proper place.

4. Recognize that there is no "right" way to participate. Children learn from experimenting. Allow them to make errors, and trust that they can solve their problems. (In this way, the process becomes more important than the solution or product.) Be ready to help, when needed, and encourage children to help each other. Be flexible enough to incorporate children's playful, spontaneous ideas into any activity.

5. Plan for children to be actively involved. (While toddlers may enjoy watching and listening to a limited extent, passive waiting is difficult for them.) Be sure children are involved as much as they are able in all aspects of the activity, including preparation and clean-up.

6. Avoid dominating toddlers' play. Drilling, quizzing, telling children what to do, making too many suggestions, or offering criticism makes children self-conscious and diminishes the value of play.

7. Introduce activities and materials enthusiastically. Prepare them so they are attractive and inviting to the children.

8. Avoid comparing one child's work with another's. Comment, instead, on what each is doing. ("I see you put your pegs all around the edges of the board." "You have covered your entire paper with purple paint!")

9. Be prepared to drop your plans and instead follow the children's lead, expanding on the play in which they are already involved.

Child-Directed Play

We have stressed throughout this chapter that the primary responsibility of caregivers, for much of the toddler's day in day care, during both child- and adult-initiated play, is to allow the children to direct the play. Caregivers need to continually follow the children's lead as play activities evolve, no matter who planned or started the activity. Leading theorists, (e.g., White, Brazelton) and developmental theories (e.g., Piaget, Erickson) suggest this approach to caregiving. Likewise, most professional texts in early-childhood education suggest the importance of child-centered programs.

Yet, perhaps in part because of the recent expansion of toddler day care, and the criticism of education in general, we hear more and more about the lack of programs that are developmental and child-centered. For example, one mother wrote extensively in a *Washington Post* article about her difficulty finding a day-care center for her two-year-old that would "let children be kids" (Solovitch, 1983). Documenting this trend has been the important and enlightening research of Suransky (1982), reported in her recent book, *The Erosion of Childhood*. She writes that childhood is a natural phase of life, but that we are eroding this life phase because of the social ideology of "schooling" which is embedded in many day-care centers. She writes:

> When we critically reflect on the reification of play that has occurred in the early "schooling" of children, we notice not only that natural play has been denied to the child but that play itself has been dichotomized into a structured, cognitive curriculum . . . and "free play," which is not free, is defined with specific adult-constructed frameworks (p. 173).

Why has this trend toward schooling and structure in toddler day care become so widespread? One reason is that parents want it. In an article on parents pushing their children to learn earlier than ever, *Newsweek* (March 28, 1983) quoted one mother who felt great pressure to assure her nine-week-old baby's admission into college, "You have to start them young and push them on toward their goal." At the ITC, some parents have asked us to teach their toddlers to read. (Responding to parents' concerns is discussed in chapter 7.)

The prevalence of early schooling may also be due to the lack of opportunity caregivers have to actually practice working in a program where child-directed play predominates. Therefore, they don't get hands-on experience in implementing programs where caregivers follow the children's lead in play. Instead, the caregivers implement programs where they are the directors of play.

Caregivers can begin to reverse this trend, if first they recognize the importance of play and provide parents with the evidence that documents it. Play is, as was stated at the very beginning of this chapter, a child's life. Once caregivers understand how toddlers play, plans can be made for both child- and adult-initiated play activities in a developmental, child-centered program. By following the suggestions and guidelines presented throughout this chapter, caregivers will be entering the toddlers' world of play. And by doing this, they will be learning how to develop programs and curricula to meet the toddlers' developmental needs. They will be helping toddlers become "vital, growing, creative" individuals.

References

Bailey, R., and Burton, E. 1982. *The dynamic self.* St. Louis: C.V. Mosby.
Bruner, J.; Jolly, A.; and Sylva, K. (eds.) 1976. *Play: Its role in development and evolution.* New York: Basic Books.

Cataldo, C. 1983. *Infant and toddler programs.* Reading, MA: Addison-Wesley.

Chance, P. 1979. *Learning through play.* New York: Gardner Press.

Clarke-Stewart, A. 1982. *Day care.* Cambridge, MA: Harvard University Press.

Cretney, L. 1972. *Play* (3rd ed.). Madison, WI: Wisconsin Department of Health and Social Services.

Elder, J., and Pederson, D. 1978. Preschool children's use of objects in symbolic play. *Child Development* 49, 500–504.

Elkind, D. 1981. *The hurried child.* Reading, MA: Addison-Wesley.

Fein, G. 1981. Pretend play in childhood: An integrative review. *Child Development* 52, 1095–1118.

Fewell, R., and Vadasy, P. 1983. *Learning through play.* Hingham, MA: Teaching Resources Corporation.

Fowler, W. 1980. *Learning through play.* Boston: Allyn & Bacon.

Garvey, C. 1977. *Play.* Cambridge, MA: Harvard University Press.

Guralnich, M. 1981. The social behavior of preschool children at different developmental levels: Effects of group composition. *Journal of Experimental Child Psychology* 31, 115–130.

Harness, L. 1979. *Staff handbook.* St. Louis: Downtown Day Care.

Hartley, R., and Goldenson, R. 1963. *The complete book of children's play.* New York: Cromwell Co.

Hendrick, J. 1980. *The whole child* (2nd ed.). St. Louis: C.V. Mosby.

Isenberg, J., and Jacobs, J. 1982. *Playthings as learning tools: A parent's guide.* New York: John Wiley & Sons.

Marzollo, J., and Lloyd, J. 1972. *Learning through play.* New York: Harper & Row.

McCall, R. 1983. The ideal response. *Parents Magazine* 58(5), 96.

Newsweek. 1983. March 28.

Read, K., and Patterson, J. 1980. *The nursery school and kindergarten.* New York: Holt, Rinehart & Winston.

Solovitch, S. 1983. Why won't preschools let children be kids? *The Washington Post,* May 1, 131–132.

Spodek, B. 1977. What constitutes worthwhile experiences for young children? In B. Spodek (ed.), *Teaching practices: Re-examining assumptions.* Washington, DC: National Association for the Education of Young Children.

Sponseller, D. 1982. Play and early education. In B. Spodek (ed.), *Handbook of research in early childhood education.* New York: Free Press.

Sponseller, D., and Lowrey, M. 1976. Designing a play environment for toddlers. In D. Sponseller (ed.), *Play as a learning medium.* Washington, DC: National Association for Education of Young Children.

Stevens, J., and King, E. 1976. *Administering early childhood education programs.* Boston: Little, Brown & Co.

Stewart, I. 1982. The real world of teaching two-year-old children. *Young Children* 37, 3–12.

Stone, L., and Church, J. 1973. *Childhood and adolescence* (3rd ed.). New York: Random House.

Strother, D. 1982. Play. *Practical applications of research: Newsletter of Phi Delta Kappa* 5(2), 1–4.

Suransky, J. 1982. *The erosion of childhood.* Chicago: University of Chicago Press.

Ungerer, J.; Zelazo, P.; Kearsley, R.; and O'Leary, K. 1981. Developmental changes in the representation of objects in symbolic play from 18 to 34 months of age. *Child Development* 52, 186–195.

Vandenburg, B. 1981. Environmental and cognitive factors in social play. *Journal of Experimental Child Psychology* 31, 115–130.

Watrin, R., and Furfey, P. 1978. *Learning activities for the young preschool child.* New York: Van Nostrand.

Weinstein, M., and Flynn, M. 1982. Developmental issues important for group infant-toddler care. In R. Lurie & R. Neugebauer (eds.), *Caring for infants and toddlers* (Vol. 2). Redmond, WA: Child Care Information Exchange.

White, B. 1975. *The first three years of life.* Englewood Cliffs, NJ: Prentice-Hall.

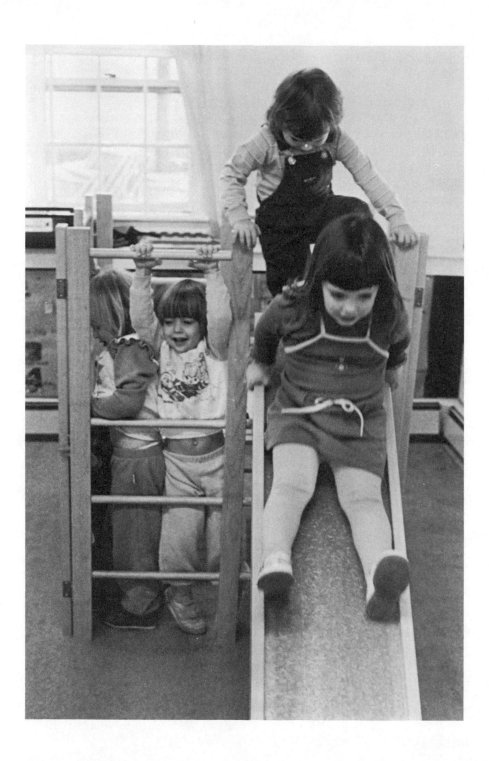

3

The Physical Environment

Setting the atmosphere where children can learn, engage in self-directed activity, talk, and discover, requires an ability to begin with a child's world and create the setting around that world.

Hutchins-Hewlett, 1978

Toddlers' play, as discussed in chapter 2, is influenced by the experiences a caregiver plans for them and by the nature of caregiver-toddler interactions. The physical environment is also a critical component when considering the facilitation of play. Researchers suggest that space quality clearly predicts differences in teacher behavior and children's responses (Harms, 1979; Kritchevsky and Prescott, 1969). For example, Kritchevsky and Prescott found that high-quality space is associated with sensitive and friendly caregivers and with interested and involved children, while low-quality space tends to be correlated with neutral and insensitive teachers, children that are less involved and interested, and a high number of classroom rules and restrictions. It is therefore important to consider carefully how to arrange toddlers' play environments.

In this chapter, we discuss both the indoor and outdoor physical environments. We examine (1) how environments can be arranged to encourage toddlers' development and enjoyment of their day-care experience; (2) how to make these environments safe; and (3) how these environments contribute to the needs of not only the toddlers, but to the needs of the staff and parents as well. Elizabeth Hutchins-Hewlett (1978) has aptly described the importance of establishing a child-centered physical environment. She writes:

Child-centered environments can be chaotic, disorganized, and overstimulating. By being designed around adult perceptions, they can operate *against* rather than *for* children. The environment in which a child spends time can and should facilitate the child. Young children's senses pick up cues in the environment in ways that adults have learned to process or ignore. Young children are unable to turn off and tune out at will as we adults have learned to do. The surroundings of a child are a stimulant for the child's behavior because of this especially alert sensory awareness. If the surroundings that adults provide for young children are not carefully organized and planned, the child can become the creature of his poorly planned environment—and in turn be denied the opportunity to create, discover, and learn about our world at an optimal level (p. 1).

A step-by-step approach follows that will help you create a day-care environment that is child-centered.

Arranging Indoor Space and Furniture

The Empty Room

Caregivers can begin to set the stage by making sure the room is large enough for all the children to play without being crowded or cramped. The National Day Care Study (Ruopp, Travers, Glantz, and Coelen, 1979) recommends that, for children under age two, the group size should be limited to eight; and for children ages two to three, it should be limited to twelve children. State licensing standards usually dictate the maximum number of children per group, and the minimum space requirements per child. At the ITC, ten toddlers were enrolled full time, and space per child amounted to more than the minimum state standard of 35 square feet.

The room should be bright, well lit, and very clean. At the ITC, we preferred to paint the walls with nontoxic, pastel colors, which provide a soft, unintrusive, and light background for children's creative displays. Brightly colored, heavy, washable curtains, combined with window shades, help to darken the room at naptime, so that toddlers fall asleep easily. Neutral colored carpeting without a pattern (to avoid a visually too-busy room) in some areas of the room will help absorb noise and allow toddlers to play comfortably on the floor.

Furniture

When purchasing and arranging equipment, keep in mind how children play, and what constitutes a safe environment. Your aim is a warm, soft, nurturing, and child-centered environment. Furniture should be child-sized. Children will get the message that this center is *their* place, and that it is especially for them. Child-sized furniture includes tables, chairs, toy shelves, and cubbies. Furniture should be washable and durable. Cubbies and hooks provide individual spaces for children's belongings, and should be low, within the reach of the children. Hooks, however, should be about shoulder level, not at toddlers' eye level, to prevent eye accidents. A couch, rocking chair, large throw pillows, small mattresses, and bean-bag chairs provide comfortable places for toddlers to curl up alone or with another toddler or adult.

A play environment works best when the room is divided into clearly defined interest centers, such as manipulative or crafts centers (see descriptions below). Special room dividers are unnecessary; furniture may be arranged to divide the room into small areas. This doubles furniture use and maximizes the available space. With distinct centers, the children know where to find specific materials, and what they may do in each area. In addition, the arrangement should be supportive of individual and small-group activities.

Maintaining the interest areas outlined in the following pages will provide toddlers with an enriched play environment. If a room is too small to accommodate all interest areas at once, caregivers can periodically rearrange centers, alternating what is available, rather than establishing an overcrowded room. At all times, however, the arrangement and materials available should encourage toddlers to be self-directed in their play choices. Descriptions follow of how to arrange space in your day-care center.

Interest Centers

Manipulative Center

Manipulatives are available for toddlers to collect, gather, dump, poke, pull, push, and so on. The materials in this area provide opportunities for toddlers to develop small-muscle coordination and hand-eye coordination. In addition, cognitive development is fostered by opportunities to classify, categorize, discriminate, construct and reconstruct. It is helpful to have this carpeted area away from traffic flow, since toddlers are likely to play with manipulative toys on the floor, typically not carrying them to a table.

A variety of manipulative toys should always be available to toddlers on low, open shelves. Avoid placing too many puzzles, pegboards, and the like on the shelves. When a few materials are simply arranged, children make choices more easily, as they can see clearly what is available. For variety, staff can rotate the materials on a weekly basis.

Caregivers can enlist the help of the children to maintain the materials in good, orderly condition, with all parts together. This is easier if puzzles and their pieces are coded, and if toys with many small parts have their own open and labeled storage containers. (Plastic dish tubs are great for this because they are durable, and the children can easily see what is in the containers.)

While most manipulatives have been designed for particular uses that promote the development of specific skills, children should be allowed to use them for other purposes, as long as they do not distract or harm other toddlers, or damage the materials. For example, some children like to stack puzzles pieces or collect and dump pegs.

Manipulative Area Materials

plastic snap-lock beads

simple puzzles, puzzles with knobs

sorting boxes

shapes boxes

pegboards with large pegs

magnetic shapes

bristle blocks

large-size legos

spools or large wooden beads to string

stacking and nesting cups

snap, zipper, and button boards

Arts and Crafts Center

Craft activities provide for free creative expression and sensory pleasures through experiences with a wide variety of materials. Fine motor coordination is also enhanced. In addition, children's language is enriched as they label sensory experiences ("Paste is sticky! Paint is wet! Playdough is soft!")

Some painting takes place at easels, set up over a washable floor, but most craft activities take place at tables for ease and convenience. These tables may also be used for dining (as long as cleanliness is maintained). If they are located near both craft supplies and water, cleaning will be facilitated.

While it is recommended that play materials should always be readily accessible to toddlers, craft supplies may be an exception. Toddlers need help with paint, paste, scissors, and sometimes with crayons. All substances should be nontoxic. Toddlers tend to taste, eyes can be poked with even blunt scissors, and paint is easily splattered. For safety's sake, as a general rule, most craft materials should be used only when a caregiver is there to supervise activities. However, daily craft experiences should be provided; and children should be able to help themselves to paste, paper, and crayons.

Crafts Area Materials

large-size crayons

blunt-edged, soft-handled scissors

colored chalk, chalkboards

large-size construction, manila, and drawing paper

fingerpaint and fingerpaint paper

watercolor and tempera paint

paint brushes of various sizes

playdough ingredients

painting easel

tissue paper

old magazines

glue and paste

Block Center

Experiences with blocks are provided to encourage creativity in construction, stimulate the imagination and encourage role playing, offer opportunities for cooperative play, and enhance large and small muscle development.

Plenty of space is required to encourage the use of many blocks in a variety of ways. Very young children tend to carry, sort, and dump blocks, before they begin to build with them. Caregivers should encourage this kind of block play, and should avoid demonstrating block building too often. Girls as well as boys should be encouraged to play with blocks.

Large, soft, foam and fabric blocks of various shapes and sizes, and sturdy cardboard blocks are most appropriate for toddlers. Hard wooden unit blocks, such as the sets found in many preschool classrooms, are less suitable, since when tumbled or dropped, they may be dangerous. Toddlers do not simply build with cardboard and foam blocks, they also carry and climb on them. Other block props such as trucks, cars, airplanes, boats, and people figures may be added to extend toddlers' play.

Smaller blocks, such as legos or bristle blocks, are best used in the manipulative area and not confused with the larger-size blocks. Toddlers like to climb inside large cardboard boxes or cases. For another activity have the children color and paint the inside and outside of these boxes.

Housekeeping/Dramatic Play Area

Dramatic play encourages cooperative play among toddlers, facilitates their language development, stimulates their imagination, and helps them develop a sense of identity and internalize the rules of their world through role playing. Boys as well as girls should be encouraged to play in the housekeeping area.

Housekeeping/Dramatic Play Area Materials
(use sturdy, child-sized domestic furniture)

refrigerator

sink and cupboard

stove

table and chairs

dolls and baby cradle

baby buggy

doll highchair

dresser

mirror (nonbreakable glass)

The following accessories enable toddlers to extend and elaborate their play:

toy food

pots, pans, dishes, kitchen utensils

doll clothes

toy telephone

clean, empty food containers (juice cartons, cereal boxes, canned goods)

small broom and mop

Given the space, time, and freedom, toddlers will spend hours in dramatic play with little direction from caregivers. As an alternative to a housekeeping center, a hospital/doctor's office, grocery stores and other real-life situations may be set up for dramatic play. Such play is most effective when realistic props are added for children to use (e.g., stethoscope, cash register).

Reading/Quiet Corner

This area is especially important for toddlers who are grouped together in day care for a long day. It provides a space for a child to be alone, apart from the group (although still supervised), when desired. When furnished with an easy chair, rocking chair, or couch, a carpet, bean-bag chairs, stuffed animals, and pillows, it is an ideal cuddling place for children and adults, as well as a comfortable place to relax alone with a picture book.

Books, attractively displayed, provide children with an opportunity to develop an appreciation for literature, and expand their vocabulary, when a caregiver reads to them. Encourage children to look at books independently and teach them how to care for them. Rather than putting out all of the center's books at once, caregivers can select certain books to be available each week. If a child asks for a specific book that is not displayed, a responsive caregiver will willingly oblige him.

Caregivers should choose books carefully for toddlers: books with bright, clear pictures, and with few words on a page. Most should tell stories about familiar situations in the toddler's life. In addition, caregivers should avoid books with sexual and cultural stereotypes in pictures, characters, and stories. Consult your public library for a current, appropriate list of books for toddlers.

Sensory Play Area

Toddlers benefit from experiences with sensory materials, such as sand and water. They can sift, measure, stir, pour, manipulate, and experiment. In this way, they develop concepts and label their experiences. A water table (low enough for children to reach comfortably), or individual tubs or trays on a table (filled alternately with water, sand, cornmeal and beans, styrofoam, and similar materials) should always be available as play choices. Rolled up sleeves and plastic bibs help protect clothing.

Sensory Play Area Materials

egg beaters

measuring cups and spoons

sand wheel

cookie or shape molds

toy boats or other objects that float

sieves or strainers

wooden mixing spoons

small scoops and shovels

Music Center

Music activities for young children are often neglected, except perhaps for a few songs before lunch or snack. However, children enjoy listening to music as well as creating their own. Music activities encourage creativity, develop auditory discrimination and language skills, and enhance motor development by encouraging rhythmic movement.

Music Area Materials

record player

recordings of a *variety* of music (include folk, classical, and pop, as well as special children's records)

tape recorder and blank tapes

wooden blocks and sticks

bells

tamborines

small drums

xylophones

autoharp

While it is safer to have adults operate the record player and tape recorder, toddlers should have frequent opportunities to play with the instruments. Caregivers shouldn't be concerned if the children's rhythm doesn't conform to the music. Toddlers should enjoy this activity (they should be happy in all their play), and caregivers should refrain from attempting to teach formal music lessons. Toddlers have to listen to a song many times before they can sing it, and indeed, they enjoy hearing one song over and over again! Records may be played also as soft background music while children play, and at naptime as they fall asleep.

Large-Muscle Area

A great deal of toddlers' play includes active movement, as they discover what they can do with their bodies. Therefore, it is important to include an *indoor* motor area to encourage developing coordination. Toddlers need room to climb, jump, slide, and walk freely. A large area should be set aside, away from the manipulatives and other small toys to prevent accidents.

Large-Muscle Area Materials

push and pull toys

riding toys

low slide

low steps

rocking horse

low climbing structure

wide balance beam

tunnel

Nature Center

This area provides objects for the toddlers to explore, stimulating their curiosity and encouraging concept development. In this corner toddlers will enjoy using all their senses to examine a variety of objects they collect on outdoor excursions, or that caregivers collect and arrange. Only a few items should be displayed at once. Having a magnifying glass handy will encourage extended interest.

Nature Area Materials (Suggested by Christine Cataldo [1983])

leaves

gourds

plants

sea shells

pine cones

tree bark

birds' nests

In addition, toddlers may observe fish or hamsters in cages of nonbreakable glass.

Evaluating the Indoor Environment

The preceding section described the components of a good play environment for toddlers. Once caregivers have set up interest centers, though, it is necessary to look at the room as a unit. Use the checklist that follows to evaluate the use of space.

1. The room is comfortable, cheerful, and aesthetically pleasing.
2. The room is safe. (See safety checklist, chapter 8.)
3. Traffic patterns are clearly defined.
4. Children move about freely with a minimum of interference and collision.

5. Furniture arrangement allows children to play alone or in small groups.
6. Interest centers are clearly defined. (Materials are not scattered around the room.)
7. Easily accessible materials encourage children to be self-directed in choosing activities.
8. Toy shelves are installed low enough for toddlers to reach and see.
9. Space and lighting facilitate the use of materials where they are displayed.
10. Each interest center contains suitable materials.
11. Children easily can see where to store materials when they are not being used.
12. Each child has a personal coat hook and cubby.
13. Quiet and active areas are separated.
14. The room includes plenty of soft furnishings: carpet, sofa, cushions, etc.
15. Children's work, or familiar childhood scenes, are displayed and are at children's eye level.
16. The room is clean and easy to clean.

The following checklist can be used to evaluate materials in your center. (See appendix B for a list of low-cost, homemade toys.)

1. Materials are age-appropriate (for example, *large*-size legos and pegboards).
2. Materials are in good condition and well organized.
3. Materials lend themselves to a variety of experiences.
4. There are enough materials, but not too many, in each interest area.
5. Materials are displayed attractively, inviting children to use them.
6. Materials vary in color, texture, size, shape, and complexity.
7. Materials can be used with flexibility.
8. Toddlers can use materials with a minimum of adult help.
9. Caregivers' supplies (e.g., scissors, soap) are convenient for adults but safely out of children's reach.

The Outdoor Environment

Having considered the indoor environment, let us now consider the properties of an outdoor environment that encourage developmental, child-directed play. Outdoor play is intended to provide children with fresh air and sunlight; to provide them opportunties to experience rain and snow; to see the sky and clouds; to feel earth, rock, grass, and trees; and to learn about plant and animal life. In the outdoors, children have lots of space for wide movements, such as running and tricycling.

The outdoor environment should have areas and equipment for large motor and sensory play. Enclosing the area with a fence prevents children from wandering off. The following is a list of appropriate outdoor equipment.

low slide

low climbing structure

baby or tire swings

sand play area

water play in wading pool or on table

riding toys

push and pull toys

soft, large and small balls

The playground should have lots of grassy areas with enough paved areas for riding toys. Shade trees should be plentiful. At the ITC there also is a small area set aside for a vegetable and flower garden.

Finances are a problem in most day-care centers. A large grassy area and an inexpensive sandbox are all you need for an adequate beginning playground. Expensive, fancy climbing structures are not necessary. Frequently they are dangerous since they are too high off the ground for toddlers. The outdoor play environment may be augmented with sand and riding toys. Larger equipment, such as listed above, may be added gradually.

When outdoors, children love playing in piles of leaves, observing birds and airplanes, watching squirrels scamper across the yard, smelling flowers, running after butterflies, jumping in puddles, and so on. Even in a "poor" outdoor environment, alert caregivers can encourage plenty of activity.

Evaluating the Outdoor Environment

Caregivers can use the following checklist to examine the appropriateness of the outdoor playground for toddlers.

1. Equipment is accessible to children.
2. Sand and water are available in warm months.
3. Several children can play on the same equipment or in the same area at the same time.
4. Partially enclosed, shaded play space is available.
5. Equipment is heavy and durable; not likely to topple when children use it.
6. One set of equipment does not interfere with the safety of another.
7. Equipment and space reflect the development and interests of toddlers.
8. There are many activities from which to choose.

A Word About Safety

Young toddlers are beginning to learn how to use their bodies in a coordinated way, as they interact with each other and with a variety of materials. This involves a lot of experimentation, during which toddlers are not always aware of their physical limits, nor of dangers (for example, of placing small objects in their mouths, or of poking their fingers into any opening). For these reasons, it is *absolutely critical* for caregivers to be alert for any dangers in the physical environment, and to make every effort to eliminate them. (Chapter 8 includes a detailed checklist for indoor and outdoor safety.) In addition, staff can invite parents to check for possible hazards. Toddlers' parents usually are aware of potential dangers, since they may have rearranged their homes when their infants became traveling, reaching, grasping toddlers. Staff and parents can eliminate toys that do not meet the criteria listed in the following checklist. Select toys that:

1. are appropriate for toddlers' age and development;
2. are *not* small enough to be swallowed;
3. do not have detachable parts, which can lodge in a toddler's windpipe, ears or nostrils;
4. are not apt to break easily into small pieces leaving jagged edges;
5. do not have sharp edges or points;
6. are not put together with exposed straight pins, sharp wires, or nails;
7. are not made of glass or brittle plastic;
8. are not made of toxic materials;
9. have no parts that can pinch fingers or catch hair;
10. do not make a lot of noise, which may injure a child's hearing.

One last, and very important, word about safety: *toddlers should never be left unsupervised*, even for one minute! Caregivers should always know where toddlers are. No matter how well planned a play environment is, accidents happen, often very quickly. There is no substitute for adult interest and supervision. (See chapter 8 for a more detailed discussion of health and safety components of toddler day care.)

Meeting the Needs of Toddlers, Parents, and Staff

Toddlers' Needs

Providing an interesting and diversified play environment for toddlers requires thoughtful evaluation and organization. A good play environment invites toddlers to explore safely. Children become involved meaningfully in play when toys and activities are offered that are appropriate for their varying stages of development and interests. Caregivers must recognize that their own behavior determines, to a great extent, whether an environment, no matter how well arranged, is or is not effective. Caregivers must trust that children's choices usually reflect their needs. Even so, just because children choose materials, it does not necessarily follow that they know how to use them. Caregivers need to play with toddlers to demonstrate how to use and care for toys, and to extend play as they engage in natural conversation. Through observation and participation, caregivers can learn from toddlers' play how to best arrange the physical environment as well as plan appropriate experiences.

Impact on Parents

Day-care staff also must realize that the physical environment has an impact on parents as well as on their children. What parents see influences what they think about the program. A clean, organized environment in which materials are accessible to children sends positive messages to parents. Parents can envision their children's daily play and activities when they see an environment organized by interest centers. A room that is thoughtfully cared for can imply that caregivers are attentive to the toddler's needs. And, of course, parents feel great pride when others see their little child's creations displayed.

We caution caregivers to avoid extremes. They should not attempt to clean up and put away everything when parents visit, since parents need to see that children are free to play with the materials. Nor should caregivers become so lax that rooms seem always to be in a mess.

When children have personal cubbies and coat hooks, parents can easily help with their child's dressing. They also can quickly spot and pick up their toddler's work and take it home.

A prominently displayed bulletin board facilitates communication. Announcements of daily activities and upcoming events may be posted. Other information of general interest to parents is readily available.

The play environment also should be set up so that parents feel welcome to observe and participate. Clearly defined activity areas and posted schedules and procedures are helpful to parents when they visit the classroom. They'll feel especially welcome if you provide a few adult-sized chairs.

Staff Needs

The physical environment influences the caregiver's as well as the child's behavior. Disorganized space and materials discourage caregivers from following through on limits, and from enhancing toddlers' play. Staff deserve furniture and space that is comfortable, and they require convenient storage for supplies that must be kept away from children. To encourage professional development, the staff need somewhere to plan and to study—a place where there is a minimum of interruption and distraction, and where resource materials are readily available. This area (library, office, or lounge) is where caregivers may take a peaceful break, and can relax before returning to the intensive interaction and attention toddlers at play demand.

Summary

We quoted Hutchins-Hewlett (1978) at the beginning of this chapter. She suggests that it is important to remember, when planning the physical environment of a toddler day-care center, "to begin with a child's world and create the setting around that world." We have stressed that, in addition, caregivers consider their own needs (for example, planning space away from the children's space). We discussed the influence of the physical environment on parents. When any one of these components (toddler needs, staff needs, parent needs) is ignored in relation to the physical environment, the other components are weakened. The ideal physical environment does not have to be large or expensively furnished. It does, however, have to be carefully designed to meet the needs of all who use it.

References

Cataldo, C. 1983. *Infant and toddler programs*. Reading, MA: Addison-Wesley.

Harms, T. 1979. Evaluating settings for learning. In D. Hewes (ed.), *Administration: Making programs work for children and families*. Washington, DC: National Association for the Education of Young Children.

Harness, L. 1979. *Employee handbook*. St. Louis: Downtown Day Care.

Hutchins-Hewlett, E. 1978. *Setting the stage for young children*. Unpublished handout.

Kritchevsky, S., and Prescott, E. 1969. *Planning environments for young children: Physical space*. Washington, DC: National Association for the Education of Young Children.

Ruopp, R.; Travers, J.; Glantz, F.; and Coelen, C. 1979. *Children at the center*. (Final report of the National Day Care Study, Vol. 1.) Cambridge, MA: ABT Associates, Inc.

4

Managing Routines Within the Daily Schedule

Time is not a line but a network of intentionalities.
Merleau-Ponty, 1962

Much research and training has been devoted to providing developmentally appropriate and educationally worthwhile experiences for young children in day care. Because of this, many new caregivers tend to think of the "activity period" as the most professional part of their and their children's day. They spend great energy preparing for the one-half to one hour of the toddlers' day when the main activity is implemented. This focus can lend itself to caregivers relegating less importance to the other seven to nine hours the toddlers spend at the center. This can result in equating caregiving with babysitting.

Experienced caregivers know that much of their time is spent in obligatory care routines, such as diapering, naptime, and snack, as well as managing the transitions between these routines and other parts of the day. How these hours are managed can be critical to the success of the day for both toddlers and their caregivers, and to the children's overall development. Consequently, the significance of the daily schedule and the management of routines within this schedule cannot be overlooked or taken for granted. Likewise, we cannot overemphasize the necessary skills and knowledge of child development that enable caregivers to manage this time appropriately for several children at once.

In this chapter, we examine the toddler schedule developed at the ITC, and present suggestions for managing routines within the schedule as they occur throughout the day. It should be noted, however, that before implementing any daily schedule, it is important to evaluate it in light of program goals and objectives. In chapter 1, we emphasized three important goals for any day-care program. These goals related to safety and health, happiness, and development of the whole child. The following are examples of broad objectives derived from these goals, which provide a framework for much of what we do daily at the ITC.

1. Create a warm, child-centered environment.
2. Encourage active exploration.
3. Develop children's self-control and self-management.
4. Develop children's competence and independence.
5. Provide for individual differences in needs, interests, and development.
6. Maximize choices for children.
7. Provide a safe and healthy environment.

It is also important to recognize, while reading this chapter, that all time sequences in a daily schedule are approximate, and that we do not recommend rigid adherence to timetables. Rather, the schedule and management of routines are used as guidelines, which are continually being adjusted to accommodate the changing, and often unpredictable, needs of each toddler. The daily ITC schedule follows, with an elaboration of how routines are managed within this schedule.

Daily Schedule

7:30 — 9:10	Arrival; self-directed play.
9:10 — 9:30	Snack, family-style.
9:30 — 11:20	Self-directed play; adults may introduce planned activities inside and/or outdoors.
11:20 — 11:30	Clean-up, wash-up, and songs.
11:30 — 12:00	Lunch.
12:00 — 12:30	Nap preparation: wash-up, teeth brushing, diaper changing, quiet book time on cots.
12:30 — 2:30	Naptime.
1:30 — 3:00	Quiet play as children awaken.
3:00 — 3:20	Snack.
3:20 — 5:30	Self-directed play, inside and/or outdoors; departure.

Arrival

As children arrive with their parents, caregivers need to greet them warmly. This point may seem too obvious to mention, but we have observed caregivers taking children's arrival for granted, without acknowledging their presence or welcoming their parents. To ease the transition from home to the center, parents are encouraged to help their child undress and to become involved in an activity of her choosing, or one which the caregiver has suggested. We have found that some parents are hurried at arrival time; however, when we explain why it is important to their child for them to spend a few minutes to help ease the transition, they are more than willing to accommodate.

Some children need time to simply watch the others play and may prefer to sit quietly until they warm up and feel like playing. A child who has difficulty separating from her parents should be comforted and reassured, and then encouraged to play, perhaps with a caregiver, until she can play happily on her own.

A smooth arrival time is possible if the physical environment has been previously arranged with toys and other materials immediately accessible to children on low open shelves (refer to chapter 3). In this way, children can choose to become involved independently, without waiting for an adult to introduce an activity. Children should continue to play with materials they select, with adults interacting and enhancing play when appropriate (see chapter 2), until it is time to clean up and have a snack.

In the early morning, at least one caregiver should have the responsibility for communicating with parents, while others care for the children. Information about, and special instructions for, each child can be noted and communicated to other staff via memo boards and verbal exchange.

Mealtimes

As snack time (or lunch) nears, caregivers should prepare children for the transition by explaining to them, individually, a few minutes in advance, that they will soon have to put their toys away and wash up for a snack. In this way, caregivers show respect for children's self-chosen work, and acknowledge children's need to prepare for changes.

Clean-up and preparation for snack will be considerably less hectic if caregivers approach children individually to put their toys away. Even the youngest toddler can learn to clean up after herself. Adults must give children *specific* instructions and see that they are followed through (e.g., "Let's put the legos in the box. Now let's put the box on the shelf.") Directions should be simple and include only one task at a time. Young children need to be shown, as well as told, how to put toys away. Toddlers also need to know that their caregivers are available and willing to assist them in their effort to clean up; their effort should be acknowledged and reinforced.

Approaching a few children at a time to clean and wash up helps to cut down on waiting time for children; it prevents their wandering; and it prevents adults from becoming confused about where to focus attention. For this to work, all the adults in the classroom need to know their particular responsibilities, so there are never too many or too few adults in the play or washing area.

To illustrate: one caregiver of the team may approach two or three children in a particular area, explain the transition to them, help them clean and wash up, and then lead them to the snack tables, or in songs or fingerplays in another area, if they have to wait for others. Songs should continue only as long as the toddlers are interested. While the first small group is washing up, a second group may begin to clean up, and so on, until all children are ready to eat, or are actually eating. At the ITC, our toddlers hang their washcloths on their own reachable and easily identified hooks (their photographs are on them). They are encouraged to wash independently, although most still need an adult's help to do a thorough job.

This approach to mealtime at first may seem somewhat complicated, and need much organization. Actually, the positive benefits of this individualized, child-centered approach make the extra thought and organization worthwhile. The adults have more control over the situation; children are more closely attended; unnecessary waiting is avoided, and children take some responsibility for themselves and their environment.

For the transition to be successful, when the children sit down for a meal it must be ready. Unnecessary waiting should be avoided—it's very difficult for toddlers! While lunch at the ITC is always prepared by the cook, a caregiver prepares snacks in advance. Before the children arrive, the caregiver who opens the center prepares the morning snack. The afternoon snack is prepared during naptime. Pitchers of juice and serving plates with finger food are ready to be placed on the snack tables when the children sit down.

One adult sits with, rather than stands above, the children at each table; she encourages the children to help themselves by passing serving dishes. We avoid getting up to do other things during mealtime. We make an effort at real conversation, in order to make mealtime relaxed and pleasant. Dusto and Olson (1982) remind us that mealtimes are important for developing skills other than those needed for eating:

> [Toddlers] observe the manners, eating behaviors, and food likes and dislikes of others; learn new words; gain new experiences; practice conversation skills with children and adults; and acquire skills used in other social acvities (p. 2).

Children are not forced to eat, or expected to exhibit behaviors that are not age-appropriate (for example, using silverware properly or sitting absolutely still). "Spills and imperfect table manners stem from a child's developing capabilities and inquisitive nature; the child is not trying to be naughty." (Dusto & Olson, 1982, p. 3).

As children finish their meal, those who are ready leave to wash up with one adult, while other adults supervise those who have not finished. As with preparation before meals, the ending of meals also is staggered. After children wash up, they are guided to an activity of their choosing; they do not have to wait until all the children are ready before beginning to play.

Child-Directed Play

Many centers schedule separate periods for "free play" and "activity time." In the former, children play as they will, and adults hover in the background, supervising usually for safety or disciplinary reasons. During "activity time," caregivers do almost a complete role reversal. Now, they take the lead, explicitly directing the children's activities. Often children do not choose how they will become involved, and they are required to participate. This description is extreme, but it is not a totally unrealistic picture of what occurs (see Suransky, 1982, for several examples). Another dichotomy exists when schedules are made with set times for outdoor and indoor play.

At the ITC, during the long morning and afternoon play periods, caregivers follow the guidelines for supporting play discussed in chapter 2. As you may recall, planned activities are offered at the caregivers' discretion. There is no set time for music, art, or other activities. Caregivers remain sensitive to opportune moments for introducing new inviting experiences. Music, stories, fingerpainting, and other activities for which children need help may be provided during this time. Children may choose to participate or not in these experiences; some may prefer to remain independently involved with self-chosen materials, accessible to them by the arrangement of the physical environment (see chapter 3). Children may also decide to play either inside or outdoors.

We are able to organize these play periods each day by arranging for staff members to take responsibility for specific play areas and activities. In addition, one adult is responsible for what we call "floating" (Fowler, 1980). The floater attends to children who may need help with play choices, a shoelace tied, or a diaper changed. The floater is in a position to oversee the entire group, coordinating the movements of the staff and children, freeing the other staff to become involved with the toddlers in their play.

By providing children with choices, we resist imposing our world on them, and become sensitive to their world and the ways they play and learn. While children can benefit from adult-planned activities, it is seldom mandatory that all toddlers participate. A play period designed like this encourages exploration, as children develop control over their environment and exercise their active curiosity. (For more information on enhancing play, see chapter 2.)

Naptime

As children finish their lunch, one small group at a time leaves to wash up and brush their teeth. Some toddlers are helped on the toilet; others are led into separate nap rooms where diapers are changed on individual cots. Caregivers remove shoes and other constricting clothing and place them underneath each toddler's cot. Then, they read short stories, play records, or sing songs to the children, to quiet them and ease the transition. The room is darkened. Caregivers remain in the room to rub children's backs; this often helps them to fall asleep. It is inappropriate to expect toddlers to lie perfectly still during this time, as they often fall asleep after tossing and turning or talking to themselves. Some children may like to have a favorite toy or blanket. Caregivers strive for a warm, relaxed atmosphere; forcing children to lie still is self-defeating and destructive.

If it is impossible for an adult to remain in the nap room, someone should check the sleeping children at least every fifteen minutes. Children who do not fall asleep after half an hour or so of rest, and early risers, may get up and play quietly. This is an excellent time for individual attention and extra cuddling; it also lessens the chaos of all children arising at once. The length of each child's nap is recorded on a memo board for parents' information.

While a particular time is set aside to insure a rest period, we know that not all toddlers are on the same sleep schedule. Sometimes a young toddler will fall asleep before lunch. This could indicate illness, which should be explored, but more often it indicates an individual sleeping pattern. When this happens, the sleeping toddler is carried to a cot and left to sleep. Upon awakening, the toddler eats the lunch she missed and then may play quietly while the other children sleep.

On the other hand, some of our older toddlers are not ready for an early nap at 12:30. These children are allowed to play quietly during naptime. This is possible because we have separate rooms for napping and playing. Older children may need a later nap and often fall asleep about 3:00. We do not attempt to keep the child awake; she is left to sleep while the others play.

Communication with parents will help caregivers learn about each child's sleeping patterns, enabling them to accommodate individual needs as much as possible. Parents tell caregivers about both regular sleeping patterns and occasional disruptions in these patterns. For example, in the morning a parent may tell a caregiver that her child woke up several times during the night. Then the staff knows that that child may need to sleep in the morning instead of waiting until the afternoon naptime. Ongoing talks with parents will also help caregivers to become aware of changes in the toddlers' schedules as they occur over time.

Diapering and Toileting

Many centers schedule particular times in the day for all the children to use the bathroom or have their diapers changed. This can be an unnecessary interruption of their play, and often an unmanageable time for the caregivers. Scheduled toileting rarely meets individual needs; every attempt should be made to avoid such a pattern (Evans and Saia, 1972).

At the ITC, we have not found it difficult to periodically approach individual children to check their diapers, or to help them to the toilet, while the other toddlers continue to play. In addition, children are not pressured to be toilet trained by any particular age. Caregivers discuss with parents children's readiness for training, and how often each child may need to be reminded or encouraged to use the toilet. Caregivers record on a memo board each diaper change or use of the toilet, as well as any irregularities, such as a bad diaper rash or loose stools. In this way, with a glance, caregivers check to see who needs to be changed, and no one in the group is forgotten.

When children who are beginning to learn to use the toilet have accidents, avoid punishing them. Circumstances surrounding toilet training may be conducive to promoting feelings of self-confidence and self-esteem or failure and inadequacy (Evans and Saia, 1972; White, 1975). Caregivers can expect children to accept some responsibility in changing wet clothes. As they help toddlers, it is important that adults be cheerful and enthusiastic, offering understanding and praising the toddler's efforts and accomplishments with words and hugs.

There are numerous advantages to periodic individual diaper checks throughout the day, as opposed to a group changing time. A toddler's play is not interrupted with a routine that involves much waiting and wandering. Children who do not need a change or to use the toilet may continue to play. Relaxed, individual attention may be given to one child, without rushing to attend to the others, who continue to play happily. Lastly, children may establish their own patterns and routines regarding toileting, and the observant caregiver can attend to each child's needs accordingly.

Day-care centers are currently under scrutiny related to the spread of diseases caused by lapses in sanitary routines (Hadler, Erben, Matthews, and Schuman, 1982). Thus, when diapering children it is imperative to employ stringent sanitary methods. (See chapter 8 for a detailed discussion of how to prevent the spread of disease caused by lapses in sanitary routines.) Day-care staff are encouraged to check their state center-licensing and health-code regulations, in addition to talking with pediatricians and public health officials. At the ITC, the following procedures are posted:

1. Change diapers on mats, except at nap time, when individual cots may be used.
2. Use changing paper under a child who has had a bowel movement.
3. Tie and place "BM" diapers in small plastic bags before disposal. (A wastebasket lined with a plastic bag is used only for diapers.)
4. Wash each child after every change, including their hands. (Children using the toilet should also learn to wash afterward).

5. Apply powder or ointment according to the parents' instructions.
6. Adults must *wash their hands,* and the children's, thoroughly after changing *every* diaper.
7. Clean the diaper mat after *each* use, using a solution of one tablespoon bleach to one gallon of water.

Departure

As the day nears an end, adults should continue to be involved with children as they play. The afternoon play period at the ITC is much like the morning, but we emphasize quieter-paced activities, as children tire after a long day. Play materials continue to be available to the children. Before they leave, we encourage children to put away their toys. Caregivers spend time straightening the play area more thoroughly after the children have gone home. Until then, we allow even the last child to continue to play freely.

Departure periods are excellent times for parents and caregivers to share information and provide each other with feedback about the children. Interesting anecdotes and news about what the children have done during the day are especially appealing to parents. Bad news at the end of the parents' workday is seldom what they want to hear—save major problems for discussions at another time (Willis and Ricciuti, 1980). However, it is important to be honest, although judicious, when sharing information with parents (see chapter 7). Staff should be scheduled so that one adult is free to talk with parents while the others care for the children.

In summary, the guidelines for routines recommended in this chapter, when implemented with forethought, knowledge of toddler development, organization, and communication, help to assure that goals for a responsive, child-centered program are met, while allowing for the day to flow smoothly for both caregivers and toddlers. In addition, day-care staff will take pride in their day-to-day job, knowing that everything they do, from monitoring naps to helping a child master a new skill, requires the knowledge and skills of a child-care professional.

References

Dusto, H., and Olson, C. 1982. *Environments for Eating, DNS 19, Nourishing and nurturing two-year-olds.* Ithaca, NY: Cornell University.

Evans, E., and Saia, G. 1972. *Day care for infants.* Boston: Beacon Press.

Fowler, W. 1980. *Infant and child care.* Boston: Allyn & Bacon.

Hadler, S.; Erben, J.; Matthews, D.; and Schuman, S. 1982. Effects of immunoglobulin on hepatitis A in day care centers. *Journal of the American Medical Association* 249(1), 48–76.

Merleau-Ponty, M. 1962. *Phenomenology of perception.* London: Routledge and Kegan Paul.
Suransky, V. 1982. *The erosion of childhood.* Chicago: University of Chicago Press.
White, B. 1975. *The first three years of life.* Englewood Cliffs, NJ: Prentice-Hall.
Willis, A., and Ricciuti, H. 1980. *A good beginning for babies.* Washington, DC: National Association for the Education of Young Children.

5
Guiding the Toddler's Behavior

Adults cannot really control children (with the exception of immobilizing some of their behavior). Children can, however, control themselves and welcome intelligent help to do so.

Staffieri, 1973

As the toddler makes enormous strides in his development he is a joy to be with, play with, and observe. But as parents and experienced caregivers know, working with toddlers is challenging—sometimes even exasperating. The caregiver needs tremendous energy and adaptability to respond to the toddler's intense and variable feelings and behavior. In this chapter, we discuss how caregivers can effectively and positively manage toddlers' behavior, a task even more challenging when one is responsible for five, eight, or more toddlers at once. Our suggestions are based on what we know about toddlers' abilities and limitations, and on our own goals for their development. We begin with a discussion of these goals and what we mean by the term "guidance." Then, we review typical behaviors of toddlers that caregivers need to accept and learn to manage. To help caregivers toward this end, we outline and explain the components of the guidance process. Finally, specific problem behaviors toddlers may exhibit are discussed, as well as strategies for dealing with them.

The Meaning of Guidance

The term "guidance" is used here to describe deliberate child-rearing strategies used by adults to elicit desired behavior from children. According to Marion (1981), two major goals govern the process of guiding children's behavior. These goals influence the specific approaches caregivers apply. The immediate goal is confronting and dealing with situations and problems that arise daily with toddlers at the day-care center. The long-term goal is to help children ultimately develop self-control and self-management skills. We want toddlers to begin to be as competent and independent *as they are able*.

It is important to recognize that adults cannot force children to behave acceptably. Because we respect each toddler as an individual—even when he displays inappropriate behavior—physical punishment, verbal abuse, and humiliation are never acceptable. When adults rely on the child's fear of punishment, the child does not learn why certain behaviors are not allowed and what would be more appropriate. A much more positive and effective approach is for caregivers to recall the uniqueness of development during toddlerhood, especially a child's growing awareness of self and his emerging sensitivity and awareness of and empathy for others. This development is all part of his evolutionary inheritance, as described in chapter 1. Caregivers also need to demonstrate respect and value for the toddler's development as a special individual with abilities and limitations. To help the caregiver gain insight into the toddler, the following section elaborates on those toddler characteristics which most often present conflicts and problems for the caregiver.

Understanding the Toddler's Behavior

The toddler works tirelessly at refining his growing skills, taking care of his needs as independently as possible, learning to communicate and comprehend the adult world from his limited perspective and experience. He is striving to become a separate person who can do things for himself in his own way. At the same time, he needs to know he is loved and will not be abandoned.

Although the toddler is developing new abilities at an amazing rate, there are still limits to this development which are related to his coordination, memory, perception, language, and thinking ability. The adult must take these limitations into account when responding to the toddler's behavior. When caregivers know what behaviors to expect from toddlers as typical and age-appropriate, it is less likely caregivers will react inappropriately or become frustrated by these contradictions in his development. It is important that the reader understand that the following are *not* descriptions of *mis*behavior, but of *typical* behaviors and characteristics that result from both limited and emerging development, and that lead the toddler to learning.

Insistence on Being Independent. As the toddler tries to assert himself, he resists forceful attempts to manipulate his behavior. He no longer passively accepts all authority. When in a battle of wills, however, he is fearful of losing face. He wants to do more for himself and is likely to resist help when dressing, eating, getting into the car, or crossing the street. Even so, the toddler still vacillates between dependence and independence (Keister, 1973; Provence, 1967). He needs to know that the primary adults in his life are close by and ready to assist if needed.

Very often this struggle for independence manifests itself in negative behavior, and protests of "No!" become a frequent response to requests (even when he may really mean "Yes" and go along willingly, all the while exclaiming "No!"). Such protests are a normal and positive developmental step, and an expression of the toddler's new ability to assert himself (Provence, 1983).

Intense Emotional Swings. As he grows, the toddler is experiencing a wide range of emotions and may change rapidly from one mood to another. He may go from feeling confident to fearful, from pleased to frustrated. For example, you may have observed a toddler happily putting a puzzle together, when suddenly he tosses it over with a shriek—perhaps because you offered to help, or because he couldn't fit a piece correctly.

Messiness. The toddler may want to do things for himself, but still lacks an adult's coordination. Therefore, he spills milk easily, and it seems more food is on the face, floor, and table than in his mouth. Even in play, the toddler's tendency is to smear, squash, spread, and toss materials.

Increased Activity. The toddler is learning by doing, which makes for a very active child! He is impulsive and into everything. This mobility often leads to collisions, as the toddler is not yet fully aware of his physical limitations or able to make accurate judgments about possible environmental hazards. It also explains why toddlers often find it so difficult to wait or sit still.

Egocentric Perspective. The toddler sees things, events, and people only from *his* perspective, having little understanding of others or their feelings. (He can be empathic as described in chapter 1, but not when he is the cause of another's distress.) He perceives his point of view as the only one, and assumes everyone shares it. When contradicted, the toddler is often confused and surprised. In addition, it takes time for the young toddler to understand that he can hurt others; that they are not just objects for him to poke at or upon which he can vent his frustration. This is often the reason behind toddlers' conflicts with other children.

Limited Language. The toddler's ability to understand and express himself through language is limited, although he makes great strides in language development during toddlerhood. Meanings adults attach to words or phrases are often different from that the toddler gives them (Marion, 1981). Phrases, such as "in a little while" or "soon" then become frustrating for both the adult and toddler. When the toddler doesn't understand an adult, he may not always say so out of a desire to please, or because his limited language skills make it difficult for him to express himself and his needs. This same inability to express himself adequately with words often leads to screaming, crying, hitting, or biting. The caregiver often must interpret the toddler's needs.

Limitations in Cognition. The toddler does not think like an adult. This means he has his own system of logic, and cannot reason abstractly. It may seem that a precocious toddler is just stubbornly refusing to understand or cooperate. In reality, while advanced in some ways, the toddler still needs time and experience to learn the adult meanings of many concepts. For example, the ideas of "truth" and "good" are vague, and to understand them, the toddler needs repeated experiences with these words in a variety of contexts in which their meanings are explicitly demonstrated. When a fifteen-month-old reaches out to touch another, caregivers are prompted to remind him to be "gentle." The toddler learns what this means when the caregiver takes the toddler's hand in her own and strokes the other child gently while simultaneously saying "gentle."

Toddlers also do not share an adult's sense of time. Their thinking into the future and past is limited. Repeated attempts to hurry dawdling toddlers are useless, as they operate in an immediate time frame. Suggestions on how to manage transitions are included in the guidelines given later in this chapter.

Anxiety When Separated. For the toddler, it is a back-and-forth struggle between independence and babyhood (Provence, 1983). For all his assertiveness and negativism, he often fears loss of love and abandonment (Keister, 1973). His feelings for important adults in his life are intense, often exhibited in clinging behavior and distress at separation, until he learns the absence is temporary and he can trust the adult to return.

Grabbing, Hitting, Biting, Pushing. These behaviors most often result from the inability of toddlers to adequately express themselves verbally and from their egocentric perspective. Such behavior *is to be expected* in children who are just beginning to learn the complexities of social interaction. A child who hits is not necessarily bad or malicious. Such incidents occur as part of the developmental process. A caregiver's reasonable reaction is one that turns these situations into social learning experiences. For while these behaviors are to be expected, they cannot be tolerated in a group setting in which caregivers must be concerned with the protection of all the children. Suggestions for setting limits and responding to such behaviors are discussed in a separate section of this chapter.

The Guidance Process

As we begin to understand the toddler's behavior, there are several strategies caregivers can learn in order to minimize conflict, and to foster the toddler's social and emotional development. These include creating a warm, nurturing, supportive, and secure environment; setting reasonable limits; and using positive communication and intervention techniques. Specific suggestions follow for implementing each of these strategies.

Creating a Supportive and Secure Environment

Supportive caregivers begin with a sympathetic attitude toward the toddler and an appreciation of his frustrations and struggles (Stonehouse, 1982). They are gentle, understanding, and have enduring patience. Good humor influences their perspective on daily events. Flexibility is important as they respond sensitively to individual needs. A nurturing caregiver is affectionate, friendly, and reasonable. Readers are encouraged to review the description of the responsive caregiver in chapter 2.

A predictable, safe environment, yet one not rigid in its structure, is a secure one for toddlers. The toddler can be very ritualistic and particular about his environment, about how things are done, and with whom he interacts. He will feel more secure when he knows what to expect. The following practices will help caregivers establish a secure, predictable day-care climate.

Guidelines For Creating A Supportive, Secure Environment

1. Introduce new staff gradually. Assign primary caregivers (see chapter 6), so each toddler can identify especially with one adult.
2. Have most new toddlers spend small amounts of time at the center initially. Some children may feel comfortable in a center from the beginning, others may need their parents to be present. Parents may withdraw gradually, as each toddler lengthens his day at the center.
3. Take the time to plan the physical environment (see chapter 3), the schedule (see chapter 4), and activities thoughtfully (see chapter 2). When caregivers, as well as children, know what to expect, the need for discipline is reduced. At the same time, however, avoid overregulating the environment. Children whose every action is dictated, who are deprived of the opportunity to make choices and act independently, may feel defiant, doubtful, and lack self-esteem and confidence (Hendrick, 1980).
4. Avoid abrupt changes in eating and sleeping routines. Talk with parents about each child's particular habits and incorporate them whenever possible (see chapter 4).
5. Prepare children for transitions (see chapter 4), a time when behavior problems are most likely to occur. Try saying: "When we finish snack, it will be time to wash," or "When you're finished with the puzzle, it will be time to clean up."
6. Minimize the time toddlers have to wait, as waiting is difficult for toddlers. To prevent problems, have activities ready in advance (see chapter

2), and arrange routines with flexibility (see chapter 4). When it is absolutely necessary for children to wait, acknowledge and try to ease the difficulty by saying something like: "I know it's hard for you to wait. It seems like a long time before lunch will be ready. Let's read a story while we wait."

7. Be sure there is more than one of popular toys. This minimizes conflict, as a child's play isn't constantly interrupted with demands to share.

8. Be attentive to the toddler when he is happy and playful, as well as when he is upset or needs help. This will enhance your relationship and teach the toddler that you are available and he can depend on you.

9. Give children choices. In chapter 2, we described how to give choices in play, but opportunities for choices arise during routines also. For example, children may decide which chair to sit in at lunch, and whether to use the blue or red cup. Let there be occasions when the toddler can say "No" and have it be okay with you. For example, the toddler may say "No" when asked if he wants more milk, or to play with playdough. Given the opportunity to make choices, the toddler may successfully exercise his independence in conflict-free situations.

10. Allow the toddler to do as much as possible for himself, giving him time to work out solutions, but also being alert to when he needs assistance. This applies to physical care routines as well as during play. Avoid rushing routines such as washing and dressing. What a child learns during these tasks is more important than a schedule or the next activity. This requires patience and flexibility on the part of the caregiver. Encourage efforts towards independence with specific comments such as:

    "You were a big help putting the toys away."
    "You hung up your washcloth all by yourself!"
    "You did a good job washing the table."
    "You found the right slot for the puzzle!"

11. Avoid expressions of disapproval, labeling, comparing children, or encouraging competition. We want children to develop good feelings about themselves and others, and to learn to cooperate and help each other. Never discuss a child with another adult when *any* child can hear you.

12. Minimize restrictions, reprimands, and situations in which the adult needs to say "No." Arrange the physical environment with activities the toddler *can* do, and in such a way that adult intervention is less necessary. For instance, dangerous or fragile materials should be out of the toddler's sight and reach.

In addition to the above twelve practices, the concept of a supportive and secure environment is extended in the following section to include establishing limits.

Setting Limits

Establishing a few limits will also contribute to the stability and security of the toddler's environment. The purposes of limits are to protect the safety of children and help them grow toward self-control (Marion, 1981). Through the enforcement of reasonable rules, the toddler learns what to expect and the consequences of his behavior.

To an extent, the physical environment can be arranged to guide and restrict toddlers' behavior (see chapter 3). However, caregivers still need to establish a few clearly defined and consistently maintained limits. The most effective limits are accompanied with short explanations of reasons when enforced, as well as consequences for violations. Weiser (1982) recommends that limits for toddlers be confined to three major limits:

1. A child may not hurt himself.
2. A child may not hurt someone else.
3. A child may not hurt the materials or equipment.

Rules that are primarily for the convenience of adults, that are difficult to enforce, and that restrict toddlers' exploration beyond the necessity of safety should be reevaluated by caregivers for their appropriateness.

Toddlers will need an adult's help in following through with limits, as they have not yet developed the ability to fully control themselves. Caregivers can teach toddlers by helping them see the consequences of their behavior. For example, when Josh bangs on the piano after being reminded: "Play with two fingers, because your fists make such loud noises that it hurts our ears and the piano keys," the caregiver should remove him from the piano saying: "You need to play with something else, since you can't remember how to play the piano gently." It is necessary that the caregiver then redirect him to another activity.

The following section reviews additional ways caregivers can teach children to respect and to understand limits, and to interact in positive ways.

Positive Interaction and Communication

Appropriate guidance focuses on what the toddler is allowed to do, rather than on what he is forbidden to do. Implementing the following guidelines will minimize disruptions, conflicts, and loss of face for toddlers.

Guidelines for Positive Interactions and Communication

1. Be a model for children. One of the ways children learn is through imitation. If you want children to pick up their toys, let them see you cleaning

up too. If you want children to learn good manners, you must also re-member to say "please" and "thank you" to them.

2. Speak in a friendly, low-pitched, natural voice. Children see through ar-tificial sweetness. Move near the child before speaking, kneel so your faces are level, and maintain eye contact. Keep your words simple and di-rect while speaking slowly. Avoid long explanations, lectures, and com-plicated directions. These are too much for toddlers to comprehend all at once. Your last few words are what they will remember.

3. Phrase suggestions and directions positively and avoid ultimatums. Over-use of "don't" and "no" becomes ineffective. When told what they *should* do, toddlers will have a clearer understanding of your expectations and be less likely to resist. For example:

Say:	Instead of:
"You need to *walk* indoors."	"Don't run!"
"Keep the sand in the box."	"Stop throwing sand!"
"Let *us* clean up together."	"*You* clean up, now!"

4. Reinforce or follow through on your suggestions with gestures and phys-ical help. Toddlers often need to be *shown* what to do, as well as told. Actions combined with words will be more meaningful.

5. Avoid teaching behaviors that may create problems. For example, if food (or anything else) is used as a reward, a child may learn to depend on it to motivate cooperative behavior instead of developing self-control and self-management skills. Also, food rewards are usually cookies or sweets, which may lead to poor eating habits and possibly obesity.

6. Accept the feelings toddlers express, and help them to recognize and to express their feelings verbally. You can do this by describing their emo-tions, and giving toddlers specific words they may use. The caregiver's goal is not to suppress toddlers' feelings, but to teach them to express feelings in an acceptable way. Try saying: "I know you are angry. Amy took your doll. Tell Amy 'No! My doll'," or "You're sad your Mommy left. You miss her and wish she could stay." Remember, it is not enough to tell a toddler to "use words." They need adults to teach them some of the specific words to use.

Positive Intervention

Modeling appropriate behaviors and maintaining a warm, caring relation-ship will help the toddler learn what is acceptable and unacceptable behavior. However, children need considerable practice in learning to control them-selves. Simply telling a toddler once what to do does not mean he will remem-ber and obey forever after. Adults must frequently intervene to help toddlers learn and practice appropriate behavior. When intervention is necessary, the focus should be on teaching the toddler what he ought to do, rather than on what he shouldn't do, as stated before. The following guidelines review positive ways caregivers can intervene and teach toddlers appropriate behavior.

Guidelines for Positive Intervention

1. Avoid making an issue of every infraction, especially with younger toddlers. When an eighteen-month-old grabs another child's toy, but that child doesn't mind, ignore it.
2. *Distract, divert,* and *redirect* toddlers who are misusing materials, annoying other children, or otherwise not playing appropriately. If Jill insists on completing Tristan's puzzle, redirect her, giving her one of her own. When Ginny is kicking the lunch table, instead of focusing on her negative behavior, distract her by saying, "Ginny, everyone has blue stripes on today, just like you have!" When Ben is frustrated because he can't go outside, divert his attention by inviting him to play at the water table.
3. Provide an alternative behavior. When a child is prohibited from an action or activity, tell him what he *can* do instead. For example, when Mary is frustrated with a puzzle and throws it, teach her to ask for help. When Seth pounds his hammer on the window pane, show him how to hammer at the hammer-peg toy. After redirecting a toddler, reinforce the desired behavior with positive comments.
4. Never hit or yell at a toddler. Adults can teach toddlers about expressing emotions, if they honestly verbalize their own feelings appropriately. If you become angry, say why calmly and firmly. "I am angry because you ran out in the street without waiting. You scared me because you could have been hurt." In addition, do not withdraw your affection to punish a child. He will not understand why you've become hostile, nor why, when you decide to return affection.
5. Never isolate a child to punish him. We have often observed toddlers being "timed-out" by their caregivers. Many times the toddler doesn't understand why he has been so suddenly whisked away from the group and told to sit for an amount of time he cannot estimate. His natural response is to try to get up. The result is often a power struggle between the child and the caregiver. Furthermore, children do not learn how to develop self-control. Occasionally, a child does need time away from the group to calm himself before returning to play. In these instances, such as a tantrum, withdrawal is used to *help* the child, not to punish him. Caregivers should be sympathetic and understanding of the toddler's emotions in these situations, as explained in the above guidelines.

6. Implement logical consequences (Dreikurs, 1968). When a caregiver finds a child behaving unacceptably, or violating limits, the caregiver can intervene in the following way:

   a) Be sure the toddler knows what is expected. Tell him specifically what he *should* be doing. When Lenny fills his container with water and spills it on the floor (usually an innocent act when a child is experimenting on the way to discovery) say: "You have to keep the water in the water table." Demonstrate, if necessary, showing Lenny how he can scoop water and empty it back into the table.

   b) If the behavior continues, give the child a choice of behaving appropriately, or of a logical consequence of the misbehavior. You might say: "You have a choice. You can keep the water in the table, or you may find something else to play with."

   c) When a child chooses to persist with a behavior you've communicated is inappropriate, you should immediately follow through with the consequence: "You are showing me you can't keep the water in the table, so you must leave and find another activity." Then, you help the child to find something else he *can* do.

When logical consequences are applied as illustrated here, punishment is not necessary. Toddlers can learn from their own actions in a nonthreatening way. The relationship between caregiver and toddler does not become a power struggle, and the child has no need to rebel. The toddler may go on to another activity still feeling good about himself.

Problem Behaviors

The process of helping toddlers learn to control their own behavior is slow. Most of the time, applying the strategies discussed in the previous section will prevent major problems and teach the toddler how to interact positively. For most infractions, it is usually enough for the caregiver to describe the behavior and implement logical consequences. Often, however, the caregiver is at a loss when confronted with a toddler who is hitting, biting, or having a temper tantrum. The following suggestions are offered to help caregivers deal with these more difficult situations.

Hitting

Remember that the toddler usually hits by accident or out of frustration, rarely out of malicious intent. He has not learned to express his feelings verbally or to control his behavior. When a child hits another, after making sure the victim is okay, hold the hitter and state camly and firmly, "I can't let you hit people; that hurt Clyde." At the same time, recognize his feelings and tell him what to do instead: "I know he made you angry when he took the hammer, but you must *tell* Clyde, 'Give me the hammer,' or ask me for help." Reassure him that you will protect him from his lack of control: "I won't let you hurt people." Tell him you'll protect him from others: "I won't let them hurt you." Before leaving the scene, make sure the child is happily engaged in play.

Biting

For the youngest of toddlers, biting is usually experimental, though sometimes teething causes a toddler to bite. In this case, distract the child and give him teething toys. For older toddlers, biting, like hitting, may occur out of frustration. Biting is dangerous and frightens both the biter and the bitten child. They need to be separated and the child who has been hurt must be comforted and attended to with first aid, if necessary. *Do not* encourage a toddler to bite back; this will not teach either child that biting is not permitted, and it will encourage aggressive behavior. As with hitting, tell the biter you will not let him bite—it hurts. Suggest to both children alternate activities.

Temper Tantrums

A child has a temper tantrum when he just can't cope any longer with too many choices, pressures, decisions, and conflicts. The frustration has become unbearable. A tantrum is emotionally and physically exhausting for both the child and the caregiver. Usually the toddler needs to be removed from the group until he can gradually regain control. Once removed, some toddlers need to be left alone, but still observed, until the tantrum subsides; others may need to be held and comforted until they are quieted—which approach you employ depends on the individual toddler. Afterwards, he needs a compassionate, understanding adult who can soothe him and acknowledge his feelings. The toddler should be allowed to return to the group, if he desires, without punishment, when he is calm.

Tantrums, hitting, biting, and other aggressive behaviors almost always result from a toddler's overwhelming frustration. To minimize such instances, caregivers need to be sure toddlers:

1. Are involved and interested in activities of their own choosing;
2. Understand what behavior is expected and are encouraged when behaving appropriately;
3. Are kept out of overwhelming situations;
4. Have an adult's help, but not interference;
5. Aren't unnecessarily thwarted by too many adult restrictions.

In addition, alert caregivers know when a child's limit has been reached: when he may be hungry, tired, or overstimulated. Then, the caregiver alters the situation to meet the child's needs. In time, tantrums and other aggressive behaviors will lessen, as the toddler becomes more skilled and learns to label, express, and control his feelings.

Other Persistent Problems

When a child's behavior is consistently annoying or inexplicable and nothing seems to help, consider other causes, such as his physical health. Might he have an ear infection? Is he teething? How is his vision? Caregivers should be alert to unusual family situations or events at home that may be causing the toddler stress. When the cause of disturbing behavior still can't be determined, all the caregivers (and perhaps the parents) need to take time to discuss the problem in depth. Written observations of the child will aid participants at this conference (see chapter 6). In appendix C, you will find questions to help guide the conference discussion. By taking a comprehensive look at the child, his environment, and the caregivers' responses, you may reach an understanding of the problem behavior and decide on appropriate action.

Summary

Guidance, like almost all other caregiving responsibilities, is based, first of all, on understanding toddler development and respecting each toddler as a unique individual. It is important to remember, as we stated in the beginning of this chapter, that adults cannot control children. However, children can control themselves; they want only a measure of guidance (Staffieri, 1973). When caregivers are knowledgeable about toddler development, implement the guidelines presented here, and take appropriate action when persistent problems occur, guidance becomes a positive challenge. The end result rewards both the caregivers and the toddlers. Guidance will not be viewed as a difficult and often negative aspect of caregiving.

References

Ames, L., and Ilg, F. 1976. *Your two-year-old.* New York: Delacorte Press.

Dreikurs, R., and Orey, L. 1968. *Logical consequences: A handbook of discipline.* New York: Meredith Press.

Hendrick, J. 1980. *Total learning for the whole child.* St. Louis: C.V. Mosby.

Keister, M. 1973. *Discipline, the secret heart of child care.* Greensboro: University of North Carolina.

Marion, M. 1981. *Guidance of young children.* St. Louis: C.V. Mosby.

Provence, S. 1967. *Guide for the care of infants in groups.* New York: Child Welfare League of America.

Provence, S. 1983. Toddlers aren't easy. *Parents Magazine* 98(5).

Read, K. 1980. *The nursery school and kindergarten.* New York: Holt, Rinehart & Winston.

Rubin, R.; Fischer, J.; and Doering, S. 1980. *Your toddler.* New York: Collier.

Staffieri, J. 1973. *What do we believe about childrearing?* Washington, DC: Day Care and Child Development Council of America.

Stonehouse, A. 1982. The challenge of toddlers. In R. Lurie and R. Neugehauer (eds.), *Caring for infants and toddlers: What works, what doesn't* (Vol. 2). Richmond, VA: Child Care Information Exchange.

Weiser, M. 1982. *Group care and education of infants and toddlers.* St. Louis: C.V. Mosby.

6

The Assessment Process

Human action is imbued with inexhaustible possibilities of meaning which fill the world in which the child exists and which she encounters in the course of growing up. It is this personal history that the child shapes through the meaning that she assigns to her experience, to the beckoning world which is an invitation to her to become a meaning-maker. We must attempt to understand that structuring of meaning, for only then can we hope to understand the meaning and consciousness of childhood.

Suransky, 1982

Assessment in day care traditionally has been viewed as an ongoing appraisal of the development of young children. From this perspective, children are compared to developmental norms or, as at the ITC, to themselves (i.e., their own development) over time. However, assessment is more than this. It is also a process for understanding the uniqueness of each child. Given these two perspectives, assessment becomes an integral part of a developmental, child-centered program. It helps us in seeing—and understanding—each child's social behavior, emotional responses, use of language, physical development, and use of materials and equipment. In other words, assessment helps us understand more about children's perceptions of and participation in the world around them.

By enhancing our understanding of children, we can be more responsive to them when enhancing play, more accurately informed when discussing children with their parents, and more aware of possible developmental delays that may require intervention or special care.

This chapter describes the components of the assessment process used at the ITC, the role of standardized assessment instruments in this process, and specifically how assessment can be used in planning for play. The assessment process at the ITC is based on knowledge of toddler development, a strong belief in the value of individual differences and the uniqueness of each child, and a deep commitment to viewing parents as partners in our endeavor to understand the children in our care. It consists of three components:

1. acquiring information from parents;
2. observing and then writing anecdotal and developmental records; and
3. developing a comprehensive assessment of each child.

Acquiring Information From Parents

When the toddler first walks through the center's door, there is little we know about her as an individual. Our previous experience with children and knowledge of child development guide our interactions initially, but the sooner we gain particular information about each child's individual needs, interests, capabilities, and personalities, the sooner we can begin to meet these needs.

Many centers have forms that parents complete when enrolling their toddler in order to provide the caregiver with some initial information. At the ITC these are called "Personal History Forms" (see appendix D) and are used to gather information on the child's toileting, mealtime, and sleeping habits; special fears or dislikes; as well as favorite interests. In addition, we gain an idea about each child's use of language, the sort of discipline she is used to, and other pertinent information. Acquiring these completed forms is the first step in beginning to know the children in our care. This information, while it will change over time as children grow and develop, also serves as a starting point for assessing each child's development.

To supplement this written information, caregivers also talk extensively with parents about their children. These talks are usually informal and take place at pick-up time, through phone conversations, or when parents come to participate in or to observe the program. Communication is ongoing throughout the year (see chapter 7). Initially caregivers seek information from parents about their child's development and unique characteristics. As time passes, caregiver-parent communications focus more on the sharing of information. The initial talks with mothers and fathers help caregivers gain a view of each child from each parent's perspective, and they help caregivers learn parents' goals for their child and for the program. Parents learn, from the start, that they are very important to the day-care staff, and that the information they contribute is valuable.

Combining the written personal history and parents' verbal information about each child, caregivers begin to understand each child's personal experiences, while simultaneously incorporating her into the group (see chapters 2 and 4). They are ready to begin writing anecdotal and developmental records for each toddler.

Observing and Writing Anecdotal and Developmental Records

Observing

Caregivers are always watching and observing the children in their care in an informal way. During play, caregivers observe children to see who needs assistance, or for opportunities to intervene with an idea or suggestion. They watch toddlers for signs of illness or injury throughout the day. More formal and structured observations are also used on a daily basis. These observations are based on an awareness of each child's interactions with materials and people. They serve, in part, as a basis for planning for play and for communicating with parents. These structured observations also serve as the initial step in writing both anecdotal and developmental records for each child.

Many benefits are gained by including observations as part of a developmental, child-centered program. Careful observation enhances our understanding of children, especially as individuals. Caregivers learn what each child is able to do, and identify needs that may have otherwise been overlooked. Information is gathered that may not necessarily be apparent, and adults may begin to understand events from each child's perspective. Patterns in behavior can be identified, and caregivers are able to see children more clearly over time (Cataldo, 1983). What is learned about the children in our care through observation guides caregivers in their interactions with children as well as with their parents.

Although observation of children may seem to be a natural and simple procedure, some training and experience are required, in order for observers to become skilled in recording their observations (Medinnus, 1976). There are many ways to approach observation and many ways to keep records of observations. At the ITC we have implemented procedures that are both practical and meaningful, given the typical caregiver's initial training and the number of hours available for recordkeeping in the caregiver's day. The caregivers keep two kinds of records of their observations: anecdotal and developmental.

Anecdotal Records

Anecdotal records (see appendix E) are brief accounts of an event, usually an unanticipated event. These unexpected events are recorded because in the eyes of the caregiver they are memorable and enlightening. Anecdotal records are slices of the toddler's life that offer insight about her as an individual. Collected over time, a series of anecdotal episodes reveals many aspects of her developmental process.

These anecdotes are often amusing and can be viewed positively. But some events may consist of what might be considered negative behavior, such as one child hitting another. A caregiver might choose to record this event, because such aggressive behavior is unusual for the child who initiated the hitting. A written record of the incident is helpful to the caregiver when she reviews the behavior later in an attempt to understand it.

Anecdotal records may be written by any caregiver anytime and anywhere throughout the day. When a caregiver observes an event, she takes a few minutes to record exactly what she saw in clear, concise language. It is important to do this as soon as possible after the event, in order not to forget details. In addition, each anecdotal record should be limited to a description of one specific incident (Cartwright and Cartwright, 1974). An ITC caregiver recorded the following anecdote. (The toddler's name has been changed here and in all following anecdotes.)

> Sam and Jonathan were the only ones up from nap. They were playing in the housekeeping area at the table and chairs, when the chair Sam was pushing fell over. I said, "The chair fell over. Can you pick it up?" Sam said, "Chair fall down, Jackie kiss." He then set the chair upright and kissed the seat of it four or five times.
>
> Jacalynn Hardesty (ITC caregiver)

We relay anecdotes to parents each day as they occur, and we talk about them to parents again during the assessment conference, when they can be discussed in a broader context. Therefore, all anecdotal records are saved for as long as each child is enrolled at the ITC.

Developmental Records

For the purpose of writing developmental records, each ITC caregiver selects three or four toddlers for whom he or she assumes primary responsibility. While the entire staff supervising a group of toddlers is responsible for their overall care throughout the day, assigning primary caregivers allows each staff member to concentrate on getting to know a few children very well, rather than trying to get to know in depth each child in the entire group (Willis & Ricciuti, 1980).

Slightly different in purpose from anecdotal records, developmental records are written at the time of the observation, as the caregiver attempts to record all of observable ongoing behavior. Daily, each caregiver chooses a time (clearing it first with her co-workers), to carefully observe one of her toddlers. She records observations when things are going smoothly, and it is possible for her to withdraw from play or daily routines for five to ten minutes. She records observations on a special form (see appendix F). Caregivers may observe children at any time during the day that is convenient (for example, while engaging in social play, during mealtime, while manipulating a toy). The accumulation of samplings of the toddler's behavior across all routines of the day tell us about her language, social development, fine motor coordination, and so on. The caregiver takes only enough time to describe what she observes, leaving interpretation of the behavior to a later time; thus, she can return to attend to the group rather quickly. The following excerpt is an example of Peter's behavior, and records an imaginative incident in his day.

Peter sat at my table during morning snack of graham crackers and milk. After taking a few bites of graham cracker, Peter held up his cracker and said, "Look, a horse . . . he's eating hay." I answered, "I see." Peter turned the cracker and said, "Now he's a monkey." "Eating a banana?" I asked. "Yeah," said Peter, "and now he's Charlie Brown." "Is Charlie Brown eating a graham cracker, Peter?" I asked. He just grinned and took a big bite of his cracker.

Jacalynn Hardesty (ITC caregiver)

The interpretation of any incident puts the observation in the context of the day, bringing to it related events and circumstances that help us understand the toddler's behavior. When writing the interpretation of the observation, the caregiver asks, "What did I learn about the child? What conclusions can I make about her development?"

From the example above, the caregiver might conclude that Peter has an active imagination with a vocabulary to express it, as well as a sense of humor. Lengthy interpretations are not necessary for each record. We collect several over a period of time before summarizing our perceptions of each toddler's development in a comprehensive assessment (see below). In a four-month period at least sixteen observations on each toddler can be recorded, if the caregivers observe each of their three or four toddlers every week. In this way, it is possible to collect a series of observations tracing the toddler's growth in all the developmental areas.

In reviewing both anecdotal and developmental records for a particular child, an overview of the child emerges. Caregivers, having seen the child respond to a wide range of materials and situations, note her interactions and specific qualities and interests. This information is central to the comprehensive assessment of each toddler.

Developing A Comprehensive Assessment

Twice a year at the ITC, caregivers consolidate all of the information they have acquired about the children for whom they have been primary care givers. For each toddler, they review all of her developmental and anecdotal records, her personal history, conversations with parents and other caregivers, and their own experiences in play and routines. This information is summarized on comprehensive child assessment forms developed at the ITC. These forms are open-ended and were developed to represent varying rates of development as normal and as a reflection of individual differences to be respected. The assessment includes specific documentation of the toddler's development in all areas as well as information about her unique qualities and characteristics.

The purpose of this comprehensive assessment is two-fold. First, it helps staff periodically stop for a comprehensive, integrated, and longitudinal examination of each child's growth and development. Second, this assessment serves as a basis for describing to parents how the toddler spends her day, and how she behaves and is developing while at the center. The result is a comprehensive picture of the child in day care: her interactions, interests, unique behaviors, development over time, and special qualities. And, by sharing this information periodically with parents, we are able to obtain feedback from them and thus refine the assessment. As a result, parents and caregivers together are able to develop quite an accurate picture of each child.

The ITC's comprehensive child assessment forms are comprised of three parts (see appendix G). In each part (using our developmental and anecdotal records as references), specific examples are included to illustrate our comments. Caregivers draw a picture of the toddler's growth and development since the last assessment, as well as how she is doing presently. In addition to their own comments, we provide a space for the caregiver to record parents' reactions and comments during the conference. This is done easily if two staff members, or the primary caregiver and the director, participate in the conference. Then one staff member can take notes, while the other is free to discuss the assessment with parents—giving them her full attention.

Daily Routines

The first part of the assessment describes the toddler in her daily routines: arrival, eating, sleeping, and so on. Parents frequently inquire about the child's behavior during these routines. In addition, children's behavior during these routines offer caregivers insight on how to manage them more effectively.

The following excerpt from an ITC assessment illustrates a caregiver's description of a toddler during a typical routine.

> *Eating:* Marco loves to eat! He gets excited when told it's time to eat, and washes up quickly. He adapted quickly to our routines and will try everything on his plate. He asks for more, usually in Italian, sometimes in English. He can use his fork well, but sometimes prefers his fingers. He can handle his cup well, seldom spilling. Marco also enjoys helping us wipe off the table after snack.
>
> Clara Pinkham (ITC caregiver)

Interest Inventory

An interest inventory comprises the second part of the assessment. In this part, the kind of play the toddler chooses and the ways in which she plays are described. For example, one caregiver describes a toddler's interest in sand play.

When outdoors, Nellie spends time in the sand—digging, pouring sand out of buckets, and shoveling it back in. She sometimes covers the tops of the [wooden tree] stumps with sand, patting it down, and then pushes the sand off the stumps to the concrete outside of the sandbox. She then uses a spoon to put it back inside the sandbox.

Jacalynn Hardesty (ITC caregiver)

Similar descriptions of water play, large-muscle activities, interest in manipulative toys, and so on, are included in this part of the assessment.

Development

The third section of the assessment involves summarizing the toddler's development in six categories: cognitive, motor, language, social, emotional, and creative. Even though we break up the developmental process this way in order to describe each child more precisely, it is still recognized that children's competence develops as an integrated whole, rather than separate pieces (Kamii, 1975; see chapter 1). Thus, while we describe a child's development in separate categories, we summarize by describing a child in a perpective of wholistic development as recommended by Stevens and King (1976).

Developmental guidelines or descriptions of the toddler's skills, as discussed in chapter 1 and found in many child-development texts, may help the caregiver determine what to write on this part of the assessment form. ITC caregivers also draw on knowledge learned from reviewing their developmental and anecdotal records. In keeping with the goals and objectives of the ITC, the purpose here is not to focus on what the toddler can't or doesn't do, but rather to focus on what she does and how. In addition, while using developmental norms may be helpful, children are not compared to a "normal" standard or to other children. The following excerpts from ITC assessments may illustrate this fact.

Social: Calvin is familiar with all the toddlers and caregivers and seems happy to be with everyone at the center. He often gives bearhugs to select children, and gives unexpected hugs from behind to caregivers when they're kneeling to change another child's diaper or washing someone's face. Calvin seems to prefer playing alone, at his own pace, and at an activity he has chosen. However, if one of the younger children comes over to sit by him and play with him, he enjoys the company and often babbles to them. He's begun to take toys that other children are playing with, but the toys don't really seem particularly important to him—when we explain he must wait for his turn, he does not protest, and happily finds something else with which to satisfy himself.

Jacalynn Hardesty (ITC caregiver)

Language: Mary speaks sentences of around six to eight words. She is able to express her emotions verbally. She uses more functional words (e.g., "up," "down," "around") and understands them. Mary sings often and enjoys humorous rhymes. Mary also repeats a lot of what she hears. She uses many expressions, such as, "Aren't you very happy?" Mary can talk in present and past tense, and can verbalize about the similarities and differences of objects she sees.

Nadine Grudzien (ITC lead caregiver)

Most parents usually agree with these descriptions and nod, "Yes, that sounds exactly like Calvin," or occasionally express surprise, saying, "I didn't know Mary could do that. At home I have only heard . . ." This, of course, leads to an exchange of observations and opinions and, as previously stated, the parents' information is recorded.

Typical Day

The last item on the assessment is a short description of a typical day for the toddler at the Center. This is an attempt to summarize the assessment for parents and to give a general picture, putting all the previous information in perspective. The following is an example of this summary.

Sam usually has an eventful day—playing and growing. His language abilities help him to resolve conflicts much quicker than in the past. Sam seems to enjoy being an older toddler, someone who is very familiar with the center and knows how the day should progress.

Jacalynn Hardesty (ITC caregiver)

Standardized Assessment Instruments

The purpose of a comprehensive assessment in day care is to help caregivers and parents better understand and appreciate the growth, development, and unique characteristics of each child. We have suggested that the information for a comprehensive assessment stems not from the administration of a standardized instrument, but from summaries of daily observations and interactions with each child and from continuous exchanges of information with parents.

The information from this kind of formal assessment is used to help caregivers structure the toddler's day to meet her various individual needs. It is also used to help caregivers monitor a child's growth and development over time, that is, the previous comprehensive assessment serves as a basis of comparison for the new comprehensive assessment. Thus, each child's assessment is compared to her own former assessment—not to overall developmental norms.

There are several standardized child assessment instruments available (e.g., *Bayley Scales of Mental Development,* 1965; *Portage Guide to Early Education,* Bluma et al., 1976; *Denver Developmental Screening Test,* Frankenberg et al., 1970) which are based on developmental norms. Often, the instruments are impractical for use in toddler day care. They may be time-consuming to administer, or require a specially trained caregiver to administer them. In addition, many standardized assessment instruments can be criticized for cultural bias or for having too narrow a focus (for example, on cognitive development). It is important to remember that children may be in day care for up to ten hours a day. Caregivers should have knowledge about *all aspects of growth and development*. One of the purposes of assessment is to help them acquire this information. An assessment tool with too narrow a focus often is not worth the time it takes to administer it.

Caregivers also need to have a continuous record of a child's growth and development because the development of young children, especially toddlers, progresses and changes rapidly (see chapter 1). Too often standardized assessment instruments are administered only once or twice a year. The results reflect single test performances and not the child's true developmental status (Cataldo, 1983). Assessments have to be repeated many times to gain the true developmental profile.

Standardized assessment instruments can be used to pinpoint developmental delays in children, and to identify similar or different populations for research studies. However, two serious problems arise in relying only on standardized assessment instruments to measure day-care children's performance. First, the results are often difficult to explain to parents in a meaningful way, and the implications of their child's possible failure in any category of performance may cause parents anxiety. Second, when these instruments are used exclusively caregivers may begin to coach children so they will perform well on the tests. Out of a genuine concern for the toddler to do well, a caregiver may tend toward formal instruction with explicit behavioral objectives that the instruments tests (for example, child will roll ball for five minutes, or child will learn to count to ten). This sort of teaching is contrary to the program's developmental and child-centered goals and orients it toward performance and content mastery. Subsequently, less time can be devoted to enhancing children's play, one of the primary purposes of toddler day care.

Using the Comprehensive Assessment in Planning for Play

The ideas for providing meaningful and individualized play experiences derive from caregivers' observations and interpretations of how each toddler uses materials and interacts with others in the play environment. Once caregivers have considered "What is this toddler thinking, feeling, doing? What are her needs and interests?" they can begin to support these interests with ideas for play experiences.

Discovering Areas of Oversight

When it is time to summarize an assessment, a caregiver may discover he or she knows little about some aspect of a specific toddler's play (for example, play with creative craft materials, such as paint or dough). The caregiver then should decide if this omission occurred because she failed to observe the child in this kind of play, or because there were not sufficient opportunities to observe that aspect of play. This particular assessment might result in the caregiver realizing that he or she needs to (1) provide more opportunities for play with creative craft materials, and (2) observe the specific toddler's play for ways to extend it to include creative craft materials.

Identifying Needs of Individual Children

In addition to pointing out caregivers' oversights, assessments can also pinpoint a child's need for more stimulation in certain areas of development. While no specific time or schedule can be set for the mastery of skills by all children (Watrin and Furfey, 1978), caregivers can provide experiences that are designed to enhance individual children's development in specific areas, based on their observations and assessment. The following examples illustrate how this can be done.

> *Example 1*: In her assessment, a caregiver notes that Molly does not get involved in block play, although she watches the other children and holds one or two blocks. This indicates to the caregiver that while Molly is interested in the activity, she doesn't know what to do with the blocks. Seeing this, the caregiver begins to structure some simple block play with this child, before attempting to get her involved in building complex structures. For example, the caregiver may bang blocks together with Molly, as she is already holding them; or fill and empty containers using blocks; and eventually stack and knock down blocks.

> *Example 2*: Tony is having difficulty with small manipulatives, trying to pick up too many pegs at a time, and unable to string beads. The caregiver wants to encourage his interest and so offers him plastic stacking rings to string on a piece of stiff clothesline. This makes it possible for Tony to master a task, as well as giving him practice with fine motor and hand-eye coordination in a developmentally appropriate way.

> *Example 3*: Carla, at two years, says only four words: "more," "milk," "Mama," and "uh-oh." Her parents and caregivers are concerned about her language development. In addition to repeating the sounds she makes spon-

taneously, labeling sounds and objects for her, and reading stories to her, her primary caregiver plans some special activities specifically geared to enhance Carla's language development. The caregiver decides to offer playdough and fingerpaint, but intends to focus on sound games appropriate to the sensory experience. She makes up chants "pound-pound, squeeze-squeeze" with playdough and "round and round, up and down" while fingerpainting, and asks the children participating, including Carla, to say the chants with her as they play a game.

Responding to the Developing Toddler

In addition to noting needs of specific children, caregivers' observations and assessments help them consciously both to stimulate and to respond to the toddlers' changing abilities and interests; they learn how to extend the children's learning experiences and when to introduce more challenging activities. The following examples illustrate:

Example 4: On one of our many morning walks to the flower gardens, the children noticed the birds singing overhead. They asked many questions about birds during the next few days. Caregivers responded to this interest by bringing in books about birds, bird nests, and some stuffed birds. A "bird corner" was set up using these materials. Magnifying glasses allowed the children to examine the materials; posters were put on the walls; the children spread birdseed and bread crumbs in the play yard.

Example 5: Aaron wandered happily around the playroom singing quietly to himself. He walked over to the block corner and began to hit blocks together and to dance while he sang. To support his demonstrated interest in music and movement, Aaron's primary caregiver planned to offer some musical play with child-sized cymbals and other instruments; she also played records and gave the children scarves to dance with. One day she brought in her guitar, letting the children touch and play it. Together, they learned some new songs.

The preceding examples show how caregivers can incorporate their assessments and observations of children into their planning. With each assessment, caregivers reevaluate the play setting, the emotional environment, and the experiences provided. It is important to realize that caregivers do not wait for the final comprehensive assessment to be written before they begin to plan individualized experiences. Planning is ongoing and daily, as are the observations and writing of anecdotal or developmental records.

Incorporating Plans into the Daily Schedule

How do we incorporate each caregiver's planning into the daily or weekly schedule? Sometimes, as in examples 1 and 2, it is a matter of observing a particular child and extending her play when the opportunities occur. However, more formal planning is necessary when several caregivers have ideas similar to those presented in examples 3, 4, and 5. At the ITC, weekly staff meetings are held for this purpose. Each caregiver comes to these planning meetings with suggestions for special adult-initiated experiences specifically geared to the toddlers for whom he or she is primary caregiver. Often, many or all of the children may participate in a given experience, even though, as in example 3, the activity is planned with the needs of a specific child in mind. At these meetings, caregivers share their ideas and then plan how they will incorporate one or two of their adult-initiated activities into each day of the following week. (Remember, as discussed in chapters 2 and 3, these activities are offered in addition to the play experiences children have through the use of materials already available in the playroom.)

By planning to introduce at least ten special activities each week, caregivers can be assured that each individual child's needs and interests are, in part, being addressed through play experiences. Planned play experiences become the basis for our curriculum and stems, not from arbitrarily imposed content/subject themes such as "spring" or "the circus," but from our knowledge of each toddler.

We started this chapter by saying that assessment in day care is used as an ongoing appraisal of the development of young children and as a process for understanding the uniqueness of each child. But assessment, as it has been described here, is even more. In toddler day care it can be, and we believe should be, the basis for planning for play—the basis for a developmental, child-centered curriculum.

References

Bayles Scales of Infant Development. 1965. New York: The Psychological Corporation.

Bluma, S.; Shearer, M.; Frohman, H.; and Millard, J. 1976. *Portage guide to early education.* Portage, WI: Portage Project, Cooperative Educational Service Agency.

Boehm, A., and Weinberg, R. 1977. *The classroom observer: A guide for developing observation skills.* New York: Teachers College Press.

Cabellero, I., and Whordley, P. 1981. *Orientation to infant-toddler assessment.* Atlanta, GA: Humanics, Ltd.

Cartwright, C., and Cartwright, G. 1974. *Developing observation skills.* New York: McGraw-Hill.

Cataldo, C. 1983. *Infant and toddler programs.* Reading, MA: Addison-Wesley.

Frankenberg, W.; Dodds, T.; and Fandal, A. 1970. *Denver developmental screening test.* Denver: University of Colorado Medical Center.

Kamii, C. 1975. One intelligence indivisible. *Young Children* 30, 228–238.

Medinnus, G. 1976. *Child study and observation guide.* New York: John Wiley & Sons.

Prescott, D. 1957. *The child in the educative process.* New York: McGraw-Hill.

Stevens, J., and King, E. 1976. *Administering early childhood education programs.* Boston: Little, Brown and Co.

Suransky, V. 1982. *The erosion of childhood.* Chicago: University of Chicago Press.

Watrin, R., and Furfey, P. 1978. *Learning activities for the young preschool child.* New York: Van Nostrand.

Willis, A., and Ricciuti, H. 1980. *A good beginning for babies.* Washington, DC: National Association for the Education of Young Children.

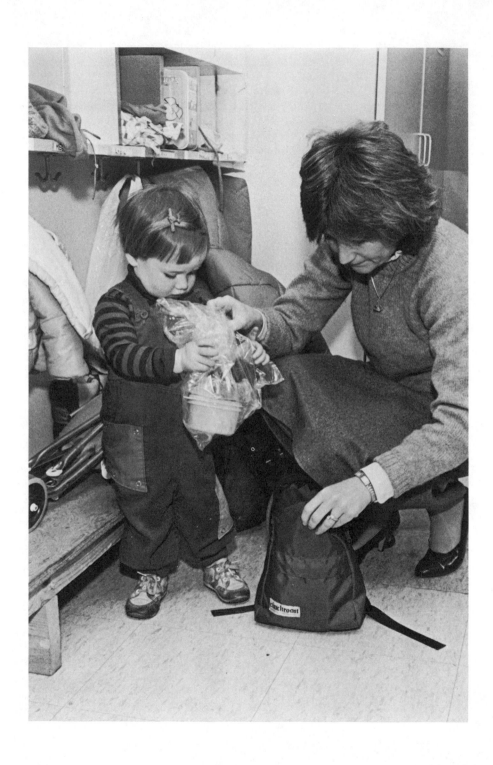

7
Working with Parents

Most of all, we believe that the needs of young children should always be considered in the context of the needs of their families—and, in particular, their parents.

Marcosson, 1978

Many times in this text, we have recommended that caregivers consult with toddlers' parents about routines, such as eating and sleeping, and the daily events affecting their toddler's health, behavior, and development. In doing so, we recognize that parents are the most important people in a child's world, and thus a valuable source of information about their child for caregivers. To best meet the needs of each child, then, caregivers should make every effort to develop a positive relationship with parents as early as possible. Because we recognize the importance of parents' well-being to a child's development we try to understand and respond to parents' concerns; to establish meaningful, ongoing communication with parents; and we explore ways parents might participate in the day-care program. This chapter discusses all of these aspects involved in working with parents.

Understanding the Special Feelings and Concerns of Parents

Both caregivers and parents nurture, guide, and foster the toddler's development. But the emotional intensity of the parent-child relationship is not present between even the most affectionate caregivers and the toddlers in their care. Thus, for parents, the focus is on the well-being of their own child. The day-care staff, however, are concerned with all the children in their care. The two differing perspectives do not have to be a source of conflict between parents and caregivers. Rather, their mutual concern for the children may lead to a positive relationship where parents' emotional and informational needs are met. The first step for caregivers in helping parents meet their needs is to understand the personal feelings which are created for many parents when they enroll their toddlers in day care. The following paragraphs describe many of these feelings.

Guilt. Placing one's child in day care is very difficult for most parents. For mothers who must work and are unhappy about it, day care is usually a less than desirable alternative. Even those parents who want to work or go to school experience conflicts in attempting to meet their own and their children's needs. Feeling disapproval from their pediatricians, friends, and family (society has not yet wholly approved outside-of-the-home care for such young children), many mothers feel guilty. When mother and father disagree, day care can become a source of conflict between parents.

Anxiety. Parents of toddlers are often more anxious and concerned about day-care arrangements than those of older children. The toddler is still very much their baby. Toddler day care is often parents' first experience with child care outside their home, and they may feel uncertain about the particular arrangement. In a recent survey (Krause-Eheart, 1984), parents expressed that one of the most difficult aspects of placing their infant or toddler in day care was in trusting the judgment of total strangers. Clearly the few, yet highly publicized, cases of child sexual abuse in day care during the summer of 1984 have exacerbated this concern.

Parents may worry that their child's needs will be ignored when in group care, and that he won't be able to communicate this to them. Perhaps never really sure of what happens once they leave the center each morning, parents may feel helpless and at the mercy of the staff. Some parents may be reluctant to express their misgivings out of fear that any questioning or criticism may be interpreted negatively by the staff, and consequently will have a detrimental effect on their child's care.

Separation Anxiety. This is often as difficult for parents as it is for the toddler. It is hard for parents to say goodbye, leaving their toddler to the care of others. Parents have expressed feelings that they miss their children very much during the day (Krause-Eheart, 1984). They miss the special time, the "firsts," the daily ups and downs. Some parents want to be there when their children need them. Other parents are sad that their toddler experiences so much that they do not share.

Jealousy. Some parents may also worry that their toddler, who spends so much of his waking time at the day-care center, will transfer his love to the caregiver, loving them less. Societal attitudes that day care weakens family bonds add to this fear. Even so, most parents want caregivers to respond to their child's unique, individual needs exactly as they would themselves. They wonder how caregivers feel about their child—whether he is liked and is as special to the caregiver as he is to them.

Burdens. Parents using day care often encounter problems which have the potential of turning day care into a burden for them rather than a service.

Some parents find that coordinating their schedules with the center's is difficult and inconvenient (Krause-Eheart, 1984). Parents are often at a loss about what to do when their toddler is too sick to attend, yet they must work. Child care is also expensive. Many parents feel burdened by the cost and effort involved with day care.

Positive Feelings. So far, we have discussed negative feelings but parents also see many positive aspects to day care. Foremost, the availability of child care enables parents to work or pursue their education. They appreciate the time they can have to themselves, to meet their own needs, while their child is cared for and safe. Parents have also expressed their enjoyment of the social contact with the caregivers and other parents. They see themselves as having learned much about parenting from the experience. Of equal importance, parents also see how participation in day care has benefited their child's development.

Responding to Parents' Concerns

Caregivers not only need to be aware of parents' feelings and concerns in relation to day care, they also need to know how to respond to parents' concerns. Caregivers need to be aware of and accept the fact that parents are all different and have individual views and behaviors. These views and behaviors may differ from those of the caregiver. However, in order to have a positive working relationship, both caregivers and parents must, as Gliedman and Roth write, ". . . relate to each other as adults who possess complementary expertise and responsibility for the child" (1980, p. 145). This relationship can be viewed as a partnership where neither possesses a monopoly on the truth and where there is give-and-take and mutual respect (Gliedman and Roth, 1980).

The ability to understand, respect, and work cooperatively with parents may be one of the hardest tasks facing caregivers. While caregivers may recognize the importance of a collaborative parent-staff relationship, many may also be apprehensive about initiating such a relationship. Caregivers may be overwhelmed at first by the different expectations each parent has and worried about how they will meet the various demands. Most caregivers want to be liked by parents, and although confident with toddlers, may feel shy and uncertain about how to approach parents. They may feel young and inexperienced compared to the parents. This can make some caregivers feel defensive about their position, procedures, and goals. In spite of these feelings, it is still the caregiver's responsibility to make an effort to know, work, communicate, and develop a caring relationship with each parent. In chapter 9 we present a checklist of personal qualities (for example, self-confidence) and interpersonal skills which can help caregivers understand their own strengths and limitations in developing relationships with parents. The following are descriptions of several times and ways to develop informal parent-staff communications.

Daily Exchanges

Greeting parents as they come to and leave the center provides one of the best opportunities for caregivers to communicate with and get to know parents. Each day, as parents arrive at the center, at least one caregiver should be available to welcome them and their toddler, while another caregiver supervises the children already there. At this time, caregivers can solicit and note information offered by the parents regarding their children. (For example, Tanya may be sleepy or cranky because she was up late last night with visiting relatives; Cory needs to be awakened early from nap to leave for a doctor's appointment.) It is essential that caregivers communicate such information to each other, especially as shifts change throughout the day. A memo board in a convenient place is especially helpful for busy parents and for caregivers. Parents and staff can write messages, knowing everyone will refer to the board for important daily information.

Caregivers can begin to let parents know they care about each child as they ask for information about each one: about likes, dislikes, eating habits, sleeping patterns, and so on. As caregivers follow through on this information, adapting the day-care schedules and activities with the flexibility we've described in this text, parents will discover that what they say to caregivers has meaning and is respected. They will begin to trust the caregivers.

Visits and Observations

Understanding the reasons for parents' concerns and questions about their children's daily experiences, caregivers can emphasize that parents are *always* welcome to stay at the center to observe or to participate at *any* time. Explaining the routines of the center, where materials are, where the bathroom is, and so on, will make it easier for the parents. It is important for caregivers to acknowledge the visiting parents' presence and interest. Sometimes we have observed caregivers ignoring parents as they sit uncomfortably in a corner of the room. When it is center policy to invite parents to visit, an effort should be made to include parents, encouraging them to feel welcome. Sometimes this means simply showing them where to hang up their coats, offering a cup of coffee, or helping them find a comfortable place to sit and observe. At other times, parents may be invited to participate in play or some activity of their choosing.

Departure Times

At the end of each day, caregivers take time to tell each parent one positive thing about their child's day. Even busy and tired parents enjoy hearing anecdotes and news about what the child did during the day. This daily communication with parents also demonstrates that caregivers appreciate and enjoy each child; it reassures and pleases parents. Again, it is important that caregivers communicate with each other so opportunities to relate events and information aren't lost. When reporting events, it is important to be honest, but no parent needs to be greeted with bad news. Incidences of contrariness and aggression are to be expected from toddlers (see chapter 5), and reports about them should be treated matter-of-factly, without judgment or criticism. Viewing and explaining incidents from a developmental perspective helps parents to better understand and to accept their toddler's behaviors.

When possible, without prying, you can also let parents know you are interested in them as individuals and in their lives. Taking the time to understand a little of what is happening in parents' lives not only helps you to develop a better perspective on the toddler's total life situation (as discussed in chapter 1), but it also helps to establish a positive relationship between parents and staff. This can only be maintained, of course, when all discussions about children and their families are treated as confidential.

Responding to Specific Concerns

For parents to feel comfortable asking questions or offering comments or criticisms about the program, caregivers need to listen and convey respect for the parent. It is important to acknowledge all concerns as legitimate. Dismissing parents' observations or concerns about wet sleeves, wet feet, cold drafts, and the like, does not reassure them or enhance your relationship. Try to honor individual parental requests with flexibility, if feasible. (This might mean arranging for a child not to play outdoors one day, but it does not have to mean caregivers will spank Alan when he misbehaves, because that's what his parents do.) When requests are in conflict with center policy, parents need to be given an explanation, not a dismissal.

Usually staff can accommodate parents' requests. At the ITC, one parent expressed her thought that caregivers didn't seem to be changing diapers often enough (her toddler had several recurring rashes). Instead of denying this, we came up with the idea to post a diaper checklist. Daily, as each child's diaper was checked or changed, caregivers noted the time and any irregularities next to each child's name on the list. This way, parents could see how often their child's diaper was changed. The staff benefited also, as it was a simple way to keep track without interrupting children's play for arbitrary all-group changing times set at regular intervals. Adjusting for most parents' requests may take some thought, time, and collaboration with other staff and the director, as well as the parents; but taking time results in improvements to program quality and parent-caregiver relations.

Being a Resource

Sometimes parents may turn to a caregiver for advice about childrearing. While caregivers can explain to parents the day-care center approaches and the reasons behind them, it is important that caregivers avoid taking over the parents' job by being overly directive. Many parents know more than they think they do and simply need the confidence to follow through on their own beliefs. Some find it difficult not to become dependent on advice from "experts." New, insecure, or troubled parents need your support and encouragement. Offer the facts you know, your observations of their children, and inform parents of the resources available to them (libraries, other parents who have had similar concerns, community agencies), but, we repeat, do not be directive. There is never *one* answer or solution to most questions and concerns.

Formal Parent-Staff Communication

Responding to parents' concerns involves a great deal of communication between parents and caregivers. In addition to exchanges of information at arrival and departure times, day-care programs can institute other, more formal, methods of communicating with parents.

Newsletters

Printing and distributing monthly newsletters is one way to give parents more detailed information about the center's daily activities. Each newsletter may consist of a few short paragraphs describing recent events, daily play experiences, and individual children's special interests. Including a favorite song or playdough recipe are added extras parents appreciate. Parents also love to see a line or two mentioning their child's name. Again, it tells them you are observing their child with special attention.

Explanations of recent policy changes and introductions of new staff are other items to be included in newsletters. Short reminders about winter clothes, center holidays, and illness policies make additional newsletter material.

Realistically, you must be aware that some parents will not find the time to read newsletters. Therefore, when you have to communicate critically important information, leave notes in children's cubbies and/or talk with parents individually. Otherwise, you cannot assume messages are received and understood.

Usually, however, most parents will enjoy a monthly newsletter. Busy parents may read them at their own convenience, as well as share them with other family members and friends. At the ITC, many of our visiting foreign parents sent their newsletters to their families back home in Korea, Brazil, Australia, and Mexico. Writing the newsletters is one way some caregivers can use their special talents and vary their day-care tasks.

Bulletin Boards

A bulletin board, hung where it is easily seen by parents, is another way to let them know about upcoming events and general information. Each week the planned experiences can be posted to announce to parents the kinds of play in which their children are involved (see chapter 2). A daily schedule and a yearly calendar are also helpful to parents. At the ITC, we also posted a bibliography of all the books available in the parent library. Information was posted about community events and resources. A constantly changing bulletin board with attractive displays is more likely to be noticed by parents than one that remains the same for several weeks or months.

Conferences

The parent-caregiver conference is a more formal opportunity for parents and caregivers to share information about each child, discuss program-related issues, or to voice questions and concerns. At the ITC, these conferences are scheduled twice a year, at which time each child's assessment is reviewed. Additional conferences are arranged to discuss assessments or other issues or topics if either parents or caregivers believe they are needed. We make an effort to arrange conferences at convenient times, when both mothers and fathers can meet privately for an uninterrupted thirty to sixty minutes with their child's primary caregiver.

It is not uncommon for both parents and caregivers to feel slightly nervous at the first conference, since it is a formal occasion. These feelings diminish significantly when caregivers make an effort to establish rapport with parents during their daily interactions. A more matter-of-fact, and even appreciative, attitude will prevail, when parents understand that conferences are regular events for *all* families, where caregivers are eager to (1) share what they have learned about the children and (2) get feedback and clarification from parents.

Parents can be put at ease while the purpose of the conference—a mutual exchange of information—is explained in a friendly and relaxed manner.

Emphasize that parents are present to express their thoughts as well as to learn in detail about the caregivers' observations. When the purpose of the conference is to review a child's assessment, first-time parents will need an explanation of the assessment procedure (see chapter 6), and why this particular approach is used. The following guidelines may help to ensure a successful conference for both the caregiver and parents. Guidelines 1 through 6 pertain to all conferences regardless of the purpose; guidelines 7 through 10 pertain specifically to conferences when assessments are discussed.

Guidelines for a Successful Parent Conference

1. Throughout the conference seek information from parents. Stop frequently to ask them open-ended questions such as: "What have you observed?" "What does Amy do when . . . ?" "What do you think about . . .?"
2. *Listen* and acknowledge parents' concerns and responses. Be attentive and show your real interest in what they say.
3. Respond honestly to parents' questions and concerns. If you cannot answer something, say that you will try to find the answer. Remember to follow through on this promise with action, and to contact the parents.
4. Do not assume parents want advice during conferences. Advice often may be interpreted as a form of criticism. Remember, parents usually know more about their child than you do.
5. Conclude conferences on a positive note. (Comment again how much you enjoy Gordie and the chance to talk to his parents.) Encourage them to continue to communicate with you throughout the year.
6. Avoid scheduling conferences too close together to prevent parents from feeling rushed.
7. Be prepared for the conference. Provide parents with a copy of the assessment that they may follow during the conference and may keep. Have a pencil to note parents' comments.
8. Refrain from handing the assessment to parents, watching them read it, and waiting for their reactions. This approach seldom elicits parents' contributions, and assumes that what the caregiver has written is all that's important.
9. Review each item of the assessment in a conversational manner. This requires the caregiver to know each assessment well.
10. Follow the parents' interests. Some parents may want to talk more about their child's eating habits, others about social development.

When problems are discussed during conferences, encourage parents to suggest strategies, and accept them if possible. This is more appropriate than the staff forcing their ideas on parents. If the parent's plan does not work out after a sincere effort has been made, it is always possible to suggest an alternative.

If a parent cannot suggest reasons for a child's behavior, or has no idea of what to do about it, caregivers may diplomatically suggest a few alternatives. Parents may then choose or modify the one with which they feel most comfortable. This approach to problem solving is a process of give-and-take for both caregivers and parents, requiring each to respect the other's expertise. Parents and caregivers become partners in decision making. This is one way that caregivers can help parents have more control over what affects their child at the day-care center. It is also a way for caregivers to acquire new perspectives on problems and issues that arise.

Sometimes, for whatever reasons, a few parents may fail to schedule a conference. At the ITC, these parents were given a copy of their child's assessment. They were encouraged to read it at their convenience and to offer comments or ask questions. Often, after reviewing what the caregivers had written, parents were impressed by how well caregivers knew their child, and they were appreciative of the caregiver's efforts. Some managed to make time for the next conference.

Parent Participation

What we have so far described in this chapter are caregivers' minimum efforts for including parents in their day care program. There are many other ways parents may become involved, including:

1. social events such as potluck dinners or picnics;
2. workdays when parents come to help clean, organize, or repair or build equipment;
3. participation in policy, budget, and other committees, or on the board of directors;
4. attendance at parent education or parent support-group meetings;
5. parent-staff meetings to discuss day-care policy or issues;
6. use of the center library;
7. saving home supplies (such as shoe boxes, paper towel rolls and juice cans) that can be used at the center; and
8. participation in program evaluation.

The amount and kind of activities parents choose depend on their particular family needs and interests. Not all parents will wish to be involved, and those who do, may not all want to become involved in the same ways. Likewise, not all staff have the same interests and special talents. Some may enjoy arranging a social event; others may prefer to spend extra time preparing for a special workshop.

There is an abundance of literature attesting to the importance of parent involvement, the primary benefit of which is its ultimate contribution to the child's development. Involvement can lead to a parent's better understanding of program goals and operations. Caregivers also begin to better understand the children and their families. Another reason for parent involvement concerns their rights relating to policies and decisions affecting their children.

These facts notwithstanding, we are finding that the needs of parents using day care differ. From center to center, and within centers, parents' interests and needs vary. Caregivers and program directors can expect different responses to their efforts to communicate and involve parents.

Powell (1977) has identified three types of parents using day care: the dependent, the independent, and the interdependent parent. Dependent parents rely on the center for information about child development and childrearing. They see the caregiver as the authority and tend to follow her advice. These parents do not take much initiative in child-related decisions. In contrast, independent parents assume that all the responsibility for childrearing is theirs, and their children are not significantly affected by the time they spend in day care. These parents make little effort to communicate with caregivers about their children. Powell describes the interdependent parent as communicating frequently with caregivers, and believing that they should share information with caregivers.

For day-care staff, this diversity among parents suggests that no specific formula for parent involvement can be directly applied at any center. For example, although most parents want to know their opinions count when decisions are being made, few want to serve on policy committees. While many parents do not have the time to participate in the classroom, all want to feel welcome there. Furthermore, we cannot assume that all parents need to be educated by us, or are ignorant about child development and childrearing practices. A considerable amount of information is increasingly and easily available to parents through articles, books, television, and community agencies.

Consequently, a lot of well-intentioned effort is misapplied when centers implement parent involvement programs without regard for the variety of populations served, and the differences in parents' needs and interests.

Foster, Berger and McLean (1981) summarize our view of parent participation when they write:

> . . . a concern for parent involvement is best shown through a point of view that continually takes into account the needs and skills of the entire family. Such a point of view does not rule out any of the current types of parent services (each of which is appropriate for many families) but rather requires that services be selected on the basis of a comprehensive understanding of a family's unique situation (p. 63).

Together, parents, staff, and the program director can determine how parents may choose to become involved. Informal and formal periodic surveys are a good way to discover parents' particular interests. Each program can evaluate, on a continuing basis, the ways parents are invited to participate. You are likely to find many parents who will participate in the activities you organize together, but many will also choose not to participate. This is the parents' prerogative. It is unfair for staff to accuse parents of not caring, when they do not respond to demands for additional involvement. Parents have multiple concerns and commitments outside the day-care center that may prevent their participation. Regardless, all parents come to the program expecting quality care. The caregiver is responsible for responding to this expectation by coordinating her talents and expertise with those of the parents.

References

Almy, M. 1975. *The early childhood educator at work*. New York: McGraw-Hill.

Foster, M.; Berger, M.; and McLean, M. 1981. Rethinking a good idea: A reassessment of parent involvement. *Topics in Early Childhood Special Education* 1(3), 55–65.

Galinsky, E. 1980. Parents evaluate the effects of infant-toddler day care. In R. Neugebauer and R. Lurie (eds.), *Caring for infants and toddlers: What works, what doesn't* (Vol. 1). Redmond, WA: Child Care Information Exchange.

Galinsky, E. 1982. Understanding ourselves and parents. In R. Neugebauer and R. Lurie (eds.), *Caring for infants and toddlers: What works, what doesn't* (Vol. 2). Redmond, WA: Child Care Information Exchange.

Gliedman, J., and Roth, W. 1980. *The unexpected minority: Handicapped children of America*. New York: Harcourt Brace Jovanovich.

Hendrick, J. 1980. *Total learning for the whole child*. St. Louis: C.V. Mosby.

Krause-Eheart, B. 1984. [Survey of mothers and fathers using infant/toddler day care.] Unpublished raw data.

Lurie, R., and Newman, K. 1982. A healthy tension: Parents and group infant-toddler care. In R. Neugebauer and R. Lurie (eds.), *Caring for infants and toddlers: What works, what doesn't* (Vol. 2). Redmond, WA: Child Care Information Exchange.

Marcosson, M. 1978. *The children's political checklist*. Washington, DC: Coalition for Children and Youth.

Miller, J.; Alexander, W.; Silverman, P.; Abramowitz, S.; and Neugebauer, B. 1980. Dealing with parent concerns. In R. Neugebauer and R. Lurie (eds.), *Caring for infants and toddlers: What works, what doesn't* (Vol. 1). Redmond, WA: Child Care Information Exchange.

Powell, D. 1977. *The interface between families and child care programs*. Detroit, MI: Merrill-Palmer Institute.

8
Health, Nutrition, and Safety

The first goal we might adopt for guiding child care policies is to avoid harm and to provide for the *physical survival* of all children. This is a minimum requirement and of the highest priority.

Clarke-Stewart, 1977

As stated in chapter 1, providing a healthy and safe environment for young children is the first goal of any day-care program and should receive the highest priority. One of the most important concerns facing day-care staff and parents of young children in day care is the growing controversy over how safe and healthy a day-care environment can be. It is well known that when people of any age are confined together indoors, communicable diseases are prevalent. However, Susan Aronson reports that "recent research findings focus on outbreaks, not on the usual state of health among day-care users" (1983a). She believes that children in day care are not at any substantially increased risk of developing infectious diseases compared with children receiving care at home. Aronson's conclusion is based on her careful examination of medical studies conducted on group child-care settings over a twenty-year period.

In this chapter, we elaborate on our belief that with knowledge of health, nutrition, and safety as they relate to toddler development, and by practicing good safety and sanitary procedures and precautions, caregivers can provide a safe and healthy environment for toddlers. In chapter 3, we discussed the importance of providing an interesting, diversified, and developmentally appropriate physical environment for toddlers in day care. We also suggested that a quality play environment invites toddlers to explore safely. Here we delineate, much more thoroughly, not only the importance of making the physical environment safe, but other safety precautions, including caregiver behaviors, first aid procedures, and accident and emergency procedures.

Before we discuss safety in toddler day care, we begin with a general discussion of health, including common illnesses among toddlers; how to recognize and care for an ill child; and how to prevent the spread of disease in day care. We continue with a discussion of a very important aspect of a toddler's health in day care—what and how she eats. We explore the eating habits of toddlers, their nutritional needs, and other developmental aspects of mealtime.

Health

Common Illnesses among Toddlers

Young children in group care are susceptible to many communicable diseases. Upper respiratory (colds, coughs, ear infections) and gastrointestinal (diarrhea and vomiting) illnesses occur the most frequently. Toddlers are also known to develop rashes from a variety of sources including, but not limited to, chemicals, plants, diapers, and medicines. Parasites, such as lice and ringworm, also infest toddlers. Most of these conditions are transmitted by personal and close contact.

In spite of conscientiousness and responsible care, toddlers sometimes become ill at the day-care center. At these times, the ill child will need a caregiver's special attention.

Recognizing the Ill Child

While the typical toddler cannot explain what "feels bad," an alert and attentive caregiver usually perceives when something is wrong and a child is not feeling well. The caregiver considers the toddler's behavior and appearance for clues that she may be ill. Her face may be flushed or pale; she may feel hot or cold. A sick toddler may be unusually aggressive, fussy or cranky, cry more easily, and she may be sleepy before naptime. Loss of appetite, diarrhea, and drooling are other indications of illness. The following list, adapted from Weiser (1982), describes some symptoms that a sick toddler may exhibit.

Changes in Appearance

watery, swollen, or red eyes

discharge from eyes

labored breathing

pale or flushed face or skin

hot or cold skin

rashes or sunburn

swollen areas, lumps, or spots

difficulty swallowing

drainage from ears

persistent sneezing, coughing, or runny nose

drooling

fever

Changes in Behavior

vomiting or diarrhea

increased urination

poor appetite

unusual thirst

rubbing or pulling ears

refusal to use some part of the body

increase or decrease in activity

irritability or aggressiveness

fatigue, sleepiness, or inattentiveness

interrupted or restless nap

excessive crying or whining

having more accidents than usual

clinging to parent or caregiver

Care of the Ill Child

A child who appears ill should be allowed to rest comfortably away from the group. You may want to take her temperature. The simplest way to take a toddler's temperature is with the new forehead thermometer tapes (e.g., Digitemp). Hold the tape on the child's forehead for a few seconds. While the temperature shown is not exact, these tapes do reveal whether the child has a fever. We do not recommend that caregivers take a toddler's temperature orally or rectally, since the young child does not always cooperate, and a rectal injury or a bitten thermometer may result (Feinbloom, 1975). If necessary, a physician or parent may take the child's temperature for an accurate reading.

As the child is being attended to, a staff member should call her parent. While not all illnesses require exclusion from the day-care center, an ill child is usually more comfortable at home. Even if the staff can take care of the ill toddler, parents should be notified immediately, so they can take whatever action they choose—whether to call a doctor, or take the child home. When caregivers are unsure whether a child's symptoms are severe enough to call her parents, remember that it is better to be cautious than to dismiss lightly symptoms that could lead to something serious, expose others to the disease, or prolong the illness. Parents usually do appreciate the caregiver's concern.

Some day-care centers may be equipped to care for an ill child, with extra available staff and separate sick rooms. In some instances, however, it may be best for the ill toddler to be sent home, for her own care, and for the protection of the other children. Dr. Esther Sleator, pediatric consultant for the ITC, has suggested the following criteria for determining when a toddler should be excluded from the day-care center.

1. *Fever.* Any degree is cause for exclusion.
2. *Sore throat.* With or without fever, the child should stay home until a negative throat culture is obtained. The child may return twenty-four hours after antibiotics are given for strep.
3. *Vomiting, diarrhea.* The toddler should have one day free of symptoms before returning.
4. *Conjunctivitis.* The child may return twenty-four hours after first treatment.
5. *Rashes.* The vast majority of rashes are not contagious. Impetigo, measles, and other contagious rashes are cause for exclusion. If caregivers are in doubt about a rash, they can request a statement from the child's physician.
6. *Other common contagious illnesses.* Toddlers may return when the contagious period is over and they feel well enough to attend.

Aronson (1983b) also lists criteria for considering parent needs when deciding whether or not an ill child may remain in day care. She asks:

> Will parents be able to take care of the child? Can they bring work home or work half a day? Will absence from work to care for a sick child result in loss of pay? Will the parent who is faced with a pay loss choose to leave the child in an unsafe child-care situation or even alone? These questions must be weighted in any caregiver's decision regarding the care of an ill child (p. 23).

Very often, for mild or noncontagious illnesses, the toddler will continue to attend the day-care center, so parents can return to work. Children with colds that are neither severe nor accompanied by a fever usually attend. Staff should keep tissues for nose wiping handy (remember, toddlers can't blow their noses), and they should wash their hands after wiping toddlers' noses.

It is not advisable to try to isolate these children; intimate exposure has already occurred, and the sick children may feel they are being punished for being sick (Aronson, 1983). They can be given disposable materials to play with, such as crayons, egg cartons, or fingerpaints. In addition to special playthings, Aronson states that a little extra love and reassurance from their favorite caregivers may be especially important to toddlers when they are ill.

Often caregivers are asked to administer medicine throughout the day. At the ITC, we follow a strict policy to give only medications prescribed by doctors. At no time do we keep aspirin on hand, nor do we give over-the-counter drugs brought in by parents, unless they are accompanied by a physician's note. By following such precautions we can be more assured that problems will not occur. In addition, we ask parents to provide *written* instructions and post them on a chart noting the amount and frequency of the medication to be given. When giving a child medication, never refer to it as candy. This is an essential part of poison prevention.

Preventing the Spread of Disease

The caregiver is responsible for minimizing the spread of communicable diseases. There are two main ways that the spread of disease in day-care centers can be prevented or decreased. The first is to follow good sanitation practices. Researchers tell us that the number and severity of illnesses among children in day care are related to sanitary practices and personal hygiene. For example, the most thoroughly documented information we have on the spread of illnesses in centers deals with the spread of illness by the fecal-oral route in centers caring for children who are not yet bowel trained. Meticulous handwashing has been shown to diminish the spread of such illnesses (Aronson, 1982; Black, 1977, 1981; Gelback, 1973; Hadler, 1980; Sprunt, Redman, and Leidy, 1973). Infectious organisms are spread primarily on the hands of children and staff in day-care centers. Black (1977, 1981) and Hadler (1980) found that serious diseases, such as shigellosis, giardiasis and other causes of diarrhea, as well as hepatitis, result when adults change diapers or prepare food without washing their hands. Again, we cannot stress enough the importance of routine handwashing with soap and water, and drying with paper towels.

In addition to caregivers' almost constant handwashing, good sanitary practices also include stringent diapering procedures (see chapter 4) and maintaining a clean environment. Toys that are mouthed should be washed daily, other toys, once a month. (Use a solution of one tablespoon of bleach to one gallon of water.) Care in food preparation and storage is also important. In addition, silverware, cups, washcloths, and cots should not be shared by children or adults.

The second way to prevent the spread of disease is for staff to follow the same guidelines for exclusion when they are ill themselves as when treating children. Often we have observed that dedicated and well-meaning caregivers come to work ill. Substitutes may be difficult to find, staff may not have paid sick leave, or they may be concerned about the consistency of care for their toddlers. However, when they are ill, caregivers encourage the spread of contagious diseases and are seldom able to give their best care. It is, therefore, essential that sick caregivers stay at home until they have recovered.

Other Health Concerns

There are some health conditions that may be less evident than illness. These include correctable conditions, such as vision or hearing difficulties (Aronson, 1982). It is important that toddlers have screening tests and physical exams to detect any possible conditions of this kind. In addition, caregivers should be alert to such signs as children's squinting, eye rubbing, inattentiveness, or other behaviors that may indicate poor hearing, vision, or other problems. It is important for caregivers to be aware of each child's health, as it affects her ability to benefit from the developmental experiences the program offers.

Nutrition and Eating Habits

A very important aspect of the toddler's health and development is related to the food she eats. Toddlers begin to establish eating habits that will persist throughout their lives (Birch, 1979; Ireton & Guthrie, 1972). In addition, caregivers often prepare the two daily snacks (and sometimes lunch) that toddlers are required to have in full day care. They also share all meals with the toddlers. It is important, therefore, to understand the relationship between the development of toddlers and their nutritional needs and eating habits.

Eating Habits

As the toddler approaches two years of age, her appetite changes. She eats less, because her growth rate is slowing. She also may seem uninterested in eating, because she is involved in exploring the environment and exercising all the new skills she has been acquiring. Caregivers need not be too concerned when the toddler's appetite varies—if she seems healthy, she is probably getting enough food. Many toddlers may not eat much at the day-care center, but consume plenty at home. In order to fully understand a toddler's eating patterns, however, parents and caregivers need to communicate about each child's particular eating habits and behaviors at home and at the center.

Nutritional Needs

Caregivers not only need to be aware of the individual eating habits of toddlers, it is also necessary for them to provide the appropriate kinds and amounts of food for toddlers, as the ability to eat wisely is not an inborn instinct (Pipes, 1977).

State licensing standards for day care and the Child Care Food Program dictate the amounts and kinds of food to be served to children in day care. A variety of foods, including meats, milk and other dairy products, fruits and vegetables, and whole grains, is the basis of a good diet. It is best if sugar, fats, and salt are kept to a minimum. While it may seem that some children don't like such wholesome food, repeated exposure can affect toddler's preferences (Birch, 1979). In general, simple foods are best, prepared in ways that make it easy for the toddler to feed herself. Some examples are:

sliced vegetables

fruit chunks or slices with *peels removed* (to prevent choking)

eggs

bite-sized pieces of meat

cereals without sugar coatings

whole grain breads, muffins, and crackers

chunks of mild cheese

cottage cheese

fruit and vegetable juices

noodles, potatoes, and rice

Special Considerations for Toddlers

Besides applying sound nutritional information to meal planning, caregivers should be aware of some special considerations when preparing food for toddlers. Some foods that are small and hard (such as candy, popcorn, nuts, grapes, or seeds) are dangerous and should not be served. They can easily be inhaled, lodge in the toddler's small windpipe, and cause choking. Hot dogs, peanut butter, and hard pieces of fruits and vegetables have also been known to cause choking. Other foods, especially for younger toddlers, may be hard to digest, such as broccoli, corn, cabbage, and celery. Toddlers also need to eat more than three times daily, as their stomachs cannot hold all the food needed from one meal to the next. Nutritious snacks are part of the toddler's basic food requirements—they are not extra treats or rewards.

It is also very important that caregivers take into account parents' religious, vegetarian, or other preferences. Children's allergies to certain foods must be noted. It is usually not too difficult to plan a menu or provide substitutions in such instances.

Developmental Aspects of Mealtime

Mealtime is more than a time for eating and getting proper nutrition, as mentioned in chapter 4. It is a time rich in sensory stimulation. The ways in which foods are presented and the way mealtimes are managed have an effect on the toddler's behavior, food preferences, and attitudes (Birch, Zimmerman, and Hind, 1980). Establishing a pleasant environment is the key to an enjoyable meal for both the toddler and the caregiver. The following suggestions supplement those offered in chapter 4.

During meals, it is best if toddlers are offered small amounts of food. A large helping may be overwhelming if a toddler thinks she must eat it all. Second helpings may be offered, but it is not necessary for the caregiver to urge a child to clean her plate. The toddler knows how much she needs—pressure to eat may lead to rebellion, a poor self-image, or obesity. A toddler's likes and dislikes will vary, and caregivers should respect the toddler's preferences and not impose their own.

Learning to feed herself is part of the toddler's larger task of learning to control her behavior. Invariably, there will be messes, as the toddler experiments with food and with her eating skills. To prevent an overly messy mealtime, some of the following suggestions were offered by R. Rubin, J.J. Fisher, and S.G. Doering (1980):

1. serve food in small amounts, including beverages;
2. use toddler-sized utensils of sturdy plastic;
3. avoid leaving food too long, as once the toddler's hunger is satisfied, she will play at the table;
4. have toddlers wear bibs and roll up their sleeves;
5. avoid serving hard-to-eat and sloppy foods, like soup;
6. (during play periods) provide toddlers with other nonfood "messing about" play—with mud, sand, and water.

If the caregiver is relaxed, understands the toddler's developmental needs, and knows her own limits, the children will also be relaxed. Meals will go smoothly, and the children will eat well and develop positive attitudes and eating habits.

Safety

Most accidents result from a toddler's normal, healthy curiosity and exuberance, and her lack of awareness of or understanding of danger. The active toddler is into everything, climbing over things, taking things apart (see chapter 1). Sometimes accidents happen so quickly, it seems impossible to safeguard a child every moment. But there are important precautions an adult can and should take, without being overly protective or prohibitive.

Safety Precautions

Sometimes, when a caregiver spots a toddler in a precarious position, he or she may decide, if the danger is slight, not to interfere with the toddler's learning experience. For example, if a toddler crawls under a table to retrieve a toy and tries to stand up while still underneath the table, she will hurt her head slightly and may come to the caregiver for sympathy. However, she will have learned to stay low until the way is clear.

At other times, though, a toddler may be likely to hurt herself seriously in play, and needs to be stopped or redirected from a harmful action. The caregiver should consider the child's abilities and suggest safer ways to play, for example, by saying, "Hold on tight," or "Sit down on the slide." Other verbal precautions can be used to redirect running, jumping, and climbing to appropriate play areas. Adults also can prevent children from sticking small toys or objects such as berries and leaves from shrubbery or plants in their mouths, nose, or ears. In addition, caregivers can demonstrate safety procedures. For example, they can show a child who has climbed high how to climb down, instead of simply picking her up and setting her down. With good judgment and intervention, caregivers can encourage safe play without restricting the toddler's explorations.

Besides verbal precautions and demonstrations, caregivers can implement other safety precautions which will reduce the possibility of serious accidents and will keep all accidents to a minimum. The following safety precautions relate to management of the physical environment and to specific caregiver behaviors.

Making the Physical Environment Safe

1. Leave rooms and toys clean and neat at the end of each shift. Periodically clean and straighten the room throughout each day.
2. Clean up tables, floor, and chairs after meals and activities.
3. Keep play materials clean. Throw away or repair toys with rough edges, broken parts, or those that are otherwise unsafe.
4. Mop up water and food quickly. Make sure chairs and tables are not sticky.
5. Cover electrical outlets with safety plugs. Keep electrical (and all other) cords out of reach.
6. Keep poisonous liquids, soaps, and medicines out of children's reach.
7. Use fences and locked gates to keep children away from the streets during outdoor play.
8. Make all building repairs immediately as needed.

Caregiver Behaviors to Promote Safety

1. Do not permit children to sit on tables or climb shelves.
2. Stop children at the curb, insist they look both ways before crossing the street; proceed cautiously and with control. Do not allow them to run.
3. *Never leave children alone* indoors or outdoors. Be alert to the whereabouts and actions of each child, whether asleep or awake, quiet or active.
4. Dispose of small objects that children might swallow.

5. Never pick up a child by the arms; this could pull her arms out of the sockets.
6. Be on the alert for potential hazards such as hot coffee, or hot water at the sink.
7. Insist toddlers wear shoes at all times.
8. Do not obstruct doorways and passageways.
9. Remove and destroy plastic film packaging for dolls, games, and other toys that could smother or be swallowed by small children.
10. Make sure all small hideouts where children can crawl are ventilated, cannot be locked, and can be easily exited by the children.
11. Know the center's procedures for reporting accidents or handling emergencies such as fires or tornadoes.
12. Finally, remember that accidents most often occur when adults are tired, daydreaming, busy talking to one another, or under- or over-estimating a child's ability. Accidents are less apt to occur when adults are rested, watchful, alert, and concerned for children's safety and well-being.

First Aid Procedures

As conscientious and careful as caregivers may be, sometimes accidents will occur. To minimize the extent of injuries, caregivers should know what action to take. It is important that at least one member of the staff have first aid training. Caregivers must realize that first aid is just that—immediate care and nothing else. In almost all cases (the exceptions being small cuts and bruises), while aid is being administered, another adult should immediately contact a physician or other emergency service.

The following section is only a brief review of first aid procedures for some of the most commonly occurring toddler accidents. We strongly recommend that caregivers refer to a text on first aid for more complete information, such as the resource we have used, published by the American Red Cross, *Standard First Aid and Personal Safety* (Doubleday & Co., 1979).

1. *Nosebleeds.* Keep the child in a sitting position, leaning forward, if possible, or reclining with the head and shoulders raised. Apply pressure directly at the site of bleeding by pressing the bleeding nostril toward the midline. If bleeding continues, obtain medical assistance.
2. *Cuts and bleeding.* Cleanse the wound thoroughly with soap and water. Rinse thoroughly, flushing with clean water. Blot dry with a sterile cloth, and apply a bandage to prevent infection. To control severe bleeding, apply direct pressure by hand over the dressing and elevate the wound. If bleeding fails to stop, call a physician.
3. *Poisoning.* Dilute poison by having child drink a glass of water or milk. Save the label or container of the suspected poison. Seek medical assis-

tance by calling the poison-control center or a physician. Do *not* induce vomiting if the child has induced a strong acid, strong alkali, or petroleum product.

4. *Burns.* Apply cold water or submerge the burned area in cold water. Cover with a sterile bandage. Severe burns need immediate medical attention.
5. *Choking.* If after a few seconds the child doesn't cough up the object by herself, hold her head down and give several sharp taps between the shoulder blades. Seek medical help if the object doesn't come out or the child has difficulty breathing.
6. *Bites.* Cleanse the wound thoroughly, cover it, and seek medical attention. If possible, contain the animal for medical examination.
7. *Insect bites and stings.* Wash the area and apply soothing lotions, such as calamine. Children who have severe reactions (nausea, dizziness, trouble breathing, swelling, pain) may be allergic and require emergency medical care.
8. *Falls.* If you suspect a fracture, do not attempt to move the child. Call for medical assistance. Observe a child who has a head injury for bleeding, dizziness, headache, vomiting, paleness, or unequally dilated pupils. These signs indicate a need for prompt medical attention.
9. *Mouth-to-mouth resuscitation.* When a child has stopped breathing, artificial respiration is required to restore breathing. First, clear the mouth of any obstructions. To open the air passage, tilt the child's head back. Both the mouth and nose should be sealed off by your mouth as you blow gently every three seconds. Continue until the child breathes on her own.

Accident and Emergency Procedures

In a life-threatening emergency situation, the caregiver's first step is *immediately to call for emergency medical services.* The appropriate emergency numbers, including the fire and the police departments, paramedics, poison control, and the local hospital should be posted by the telephone. When phoning in an emergency:

1. Give the nature of the emergency.
2. Give your name, address (including nearest cross street), and telephone number.
3. Do not hang up until the person on the other end has hung up.

While someone is calling the emergency numbers, another caregiver can administer first aid; the victim should not be left alone. Other staff persons should take care of the other children. The victim's parents should be notified as soon as possible. Later, injury reports should be completed by the persons who attended the child and witnessed the accident.

Robertson (1980) reviews what caregivers should do in less urgent situations still requiring medical attention:

1. Apply immediate first aid care.
2. Keep the child lying down and comfortable.
3. Call parent(s), or call alternative name listed on the child's emergency card, if parents cannot be reached.
4. Stay with the child until her parent arrives.
5. Be sure another adult attends to the other children until the emergency is over.
6. Complete an accident/illness report in duplicate. Give one copy to the parent; file the other with the child's records.

Accidents are very scary for all the adults and children involved. It is important for caregivers to remain calm and in control. Toddlers are quick to pick up on an adult's hysteria or panic. One caregiver should talk reassuringly to the victim, while another talks to the the other children, explaining that the toddler is hurt and that the adult is taking care of her to help make her better. Do not try to deny to the other children that something serious has happened. In most cases, they have witnessed the event and may be startled or frightened. While they may not be able to articulate their fears or questions, toddlers need an adult to explain the situation simply to them, reassuring them that their caregivers are there to take care of and protect them.

Conclusion

To be healthy and safe is a basic human need. The caregiver's responsibility in helping to meet this need is critically important. If this responsibility is taken lightly, all else in the day-care program, no matter how well planned, is likely to fail, for play and participation in daily routines require children who are healthy and happy. A sick child, a child who is hungry, or a child who is in pain from an accident, cannot play, and may have difficulty eating or sleeping.

Toddlers, however, do get sick; they do have accidents; and they do experience a change in appetite while establishing the beginnings of lifelong eating habits. Caregivers can minimize accidents and a child's risk of getting sick in day care as well as meet the nutritional needs of toddlers. They can do this by getting to know the individual children—the one who is always careful, the one who is usually careless, the one who loves to eat, and the one who seems to eat very little—and by understanding toddler development in general. In addition, they need to practice sound safety and sanitary precautions at all times, based on their knowledge of the individual and of the group. By minimizing the risks of illness and accidents, caregivers are simultaneously maximizing the potential for the day-care environment to be enriching for both the toddlers and for themselves.

References

American Red Cross 1979. *Standard first aid and personal safety.* Garden City, NY: Doubleday & Co.

Aronson, S. 1982. Health and safety in the child care program—an update. In R. Lurie & R. Neugebauer (eds.), *Caring for infants and toddlers: What works, What doesn't.* (Vol. 2). Redmond, WA: Child Care Information Exchange.

Aronson, S. 1983a. Infection and day care. *Child Care Information Exchange* 10 (March/April).

Aronson, S. 1983b. Health update: How sick is sick? Managing minor illnesses. *Child Care Information Exchange* 10 (November), 22–24.

Black, R. 1977. Giardiasis in day care centers: Evidence of person-to-person transmission. *Pediatrics* 60, 486.

Black, R. 1981. Handwashing to prevent diarrhea in day care centers. *Journal of Epidemiology* 113, 445–451.

Birch, L.L. 1979. Dimensions of preschool children's food preferences. *Journal of Nutrition Education* 11, 77–80.

Birch, L.L.; Zimmerman, S.I.; and Hind, H. 1980. The influence of social affective context on the formation of children's food preferences. *Child Development* 51, 856–861.

Clarke-Stewart, A. 1977. *Child care in the family: A review of research and some propositions for policy.* New York: Academic Press.

Dusto, H., and Olson, C. 1982. *Nourishing and nurturing two-year-olds.* Ithaca, NY: Cornell University Press.

Feinbloom, R., and the Boston Children's Medical Center. 1975. *Child health encyclopedia.* New York: Bell Publishing Co.

Gelback, S. 1973. Spread of disease by fecal-oral route in day nurseries. *Health Services Reports* 88, 320–322.

Hadler, M. 1980. Hepatitis A in day care centers. *New England Journal of Medicine* 1222.

Hendrick, J. 1980. *Total learning.* St. Louis: C.V. Mosby.

Ireton, C.L., and Guthrie, H.A. 1972. Modification of vegetable-eating behavior in preschool children. *Journal of Nutrition Education* 4, 100–103.

Pipes, D.L. 1977. *Nutrition in infancy and childhood.* St. Louis: C.V. Mosby.

Robertson, A. 1980. *Health, safety, and first aid training guide.* St. Paul, MN: Toys 'n' Things Training and Resource Center, Inc.

Rubin, R.R.; Fisher, J.J.; and Doering, S.G. 1980. *Your toddler.* New York: Collier Books.

Sprunt, K.; Redman, W.; and Leidy, G. 1973. Antibacterial effectiveness of routine handwashing. *Pediatrics* 52(2), 264.

Weiser, M.G. 1982. *Group care and education of infants and toddlers.* St. Louis: C.V. Mosby.

9
The Caregiver as a Professional

Within the field [of day care], we need to continue to try to increase
our own understanding of who and what we are and to feel more confident about our contributions to the welfare of children and families.
Caldwell, 1983

Throughout this book we have reviewed information, described characteristics, and outlined strategies, which, when applied, contribute
to quality caregiving for toddlers. While we have tried to be comprehensive, we must acknowledge that there is more to caregiving than we have
written, some of which is undefinable, and which can only be determined by
you, the caregiver. Who you are as an individual, and the special qualities,
talents, and insights you bring to any program, will affect the program and
make the difference when applying what you have learned from this text
about toddlers and responsive care.

In this chapter, we describe some of the essence of the professional caregiver. We have so far examined what being a professional means in relation to
our daily interactions with children and their parents. What follows is a discussion of the commitment and responsibility involved in being a child-care
professional.

What Is a Professional?

William Ade (1982) writes that, "professional status connotes specialized
knowledge, a desirable service, and an assurance of quality, dependability,
and effectiveness" (p. 25). Caregivers' specialized knowledge includes: information and understanding about child development, knowing how children
learn, implementing ways to foster their development, and understanding
each child as an individual. It also includes an awareness of programming,
issues related to group care, and interpersonal relations.

The number of children in day care attests to the fact that caregivers provide an essential service. However, this alone with professional knowledge is
not enough to represent professional status. The professional caregiver also
must ensure his or her own "quality, dependability, and effectiveness." The

individuals caring for young children must provide care that is reliable, consistent, and which fosters health, happiness, and the development of children.

Personal qualities caregivers bring to a center are also indicative of our professionalism. The following is a list of these qualities that directly or indirectly may affect a program. They serve as a checklist for caregivers to help them understand their own strengths and limitations.

Personal Qualities of Professional Caregivers

Concern for the welfare of children

Enjoyment of children

Sense of humor

Self-confidence

Flexibility and adaptability

Ability to accept and offer criticism

Openness to learning

Emotional maturity

Patience and stamina

Ability to keep information confidential

Awareness of the multicultural nature of society

Development of these characteristics will enhance relationships with children and will facilitate satisfactory relations with other adults. When you lack one of these qualities, all of your remaining qualities are simultaneously weakened.

Working with Other Caregivers

Being a caregiver involves intense and close work with children and other adults. Caregivers seldom work alone. They are usually members of a team consisting of parents and other professionals. To a great extent, a satisfying working and social atmosphere depends on the program's administrator. She or he determines the degree of staff participation in decision making, the amount and kind of feedback and support given to staff, and the program and personnel policies. These all influence the character of the program.

Each caregiver also is responsible for contributing to the professionalism of the program. This requires many interpersonal skills, some of which are listed below.

1. ability to communicate feelings without making judgments;
2. ability to listen to others;
3. respect for, and tolerance of, differences of opinion;
4. knowing *when* to say what's on your mind, as well as how;
5. acceptance of others' styles of caregiving, interaction, and their strengths and weaknesses.

All of us behave in relation to each other, and this necessitates thinking about how we initiate and respond to verbal and nonverbal communications. This does not mean that the atmosphere is stiff and formal. On the contrary, an air of relaxed openness, combined with sensitivity toward others, facilitates positive relationships among staff, children, and parents.

Because of the intense, close personal contact in day-care centers, conflicts inevitably arise and must be attended to. Usually, such conflicts result from misunderstandings or lack of communication. Before such conflicts are blown out of proportion or affect the care given to the children, the individuals involved must take the time to talk with each other and clear the air. At no time is it appropriate to take in-center grievances to the parents or discuss them with other staff while they are providing care. Such actions only negatively affect parents' confidence in the program and aggravate staff relations. Learning the skills suggested previously should be helpful in resolving conflicts.

Continued Growth and Learning

If we refer back to the definition of professionalism, we recall that attaining "specialized knowledge" and maintaining an "openness to learning" are essential components of professional quality care. The information we have about child development and the issues involved in programs for group care is not a single, static body of knowledge. Thus, it is necessary for the caregiver continuously to expand upon what has been learned from this text, or from any degree or credentialing program. Research, and our own experience, tells us that the training, education, and preparation of the caregiver does make a difference. The most recent and compelling evidence linking caregiver training to the provision of quality care comes from the findings of the National Day Care Home Study (Divine-Hawkins, 1981). This study found that the effects of training were "strong and positive." With this growing evidence, we believe that the learning process should continue throughout a caregiver's career.

Some day-care centers offer inservice training for their caregivers on a variety of topics, from guiding children's behavior to first aid. Even informal discussions during staff meetings may contribute to a caregiver's greater awareness and insight. Some administrators work with staff members individually, helping them to evaluate and improve their skills.

The staff of many centers, though, seem to have difficulty finding time and resources to coordinate and attend inservice workshops and seminars. Caregivers can take advantage of available resources in local community agencies (libraries, extension services, and community colleges); and can join professional organizations and associations on local, state, regional, or national levels (see appendix H). In addition to periodic conferences, many of these organizations publish newsletters or journals with information relevant to caregivers.

For the most part, though, the individual caregiver will need to take the initiative in exploring new information and ideas that will enhance his or her caregiving abilities. A good place to begin is by reviewing the references used for this text, and the sources listed in appendix H. Or perhaps you are already aware of your particular needs or interests. Your willingness to commit time and energy on the children's and your own behalf and to learn more will result in improvements in quality of care and your own job satisfaction.

Advocacy

Adults who care for and about children must, out of necessity and professional obligation, be concerned about political advocacy. Children have no voice themselves in the political process and must depend on adults to act for them. To be a children's advocate means to actively support policies, programs, and legislation that have a positive impact on the lives of children and their families.

The Need

You may feel that advocacy is not an issue that applies to you. You are not interested in politics. You simply want to work directly with children and their families. Nevertheless, you must realize that child care is political, and that public policy directly and indirectly affects what happens to the children in your care, to the children without programs who need them, and to you, the professional. The activities of the legislature may seem remote, until a law affects you or your program. The state and federal governments play an ever-increasing role in the lives of children and their families in the areas of funding, certification, licensing, program services, and program evaluation. Legislation designed to affect the lives of children will also affect the professionals involved in children's programs. And so we realize that both children's lives and our own lives as professionals are dependent on the advocacy activities of our profession.

To further stress the need for advocacy efforts, the Children's Defense Fund (1982) has outlined the effects of reductions in aid to children's programs:

1. lower quality child-care services;
2. fewer child-care slots for low-income and working parents;
3. fewer support services for teenage parents and parents of special needs children;
4. parents giving up hope for a better future;
5. more "latchkey" children;
6. more unsupervised children in trouble;
7. more children placed unnecessarily in costly out-of-home and institutional settings;
8. more and more children growing up without care and guidance.

In addition to the serious implications for children and their families, a lack of advocacy effort may result in the persistence of low status and low pay for the committed, qualified, and hard-working child-care professional.

What You Can Do

At this point, you may wonder what role you play in this controversy. What can one person do? Where does one begin? For many of us, the political process is unfamiliar and somewhat intimidating. With time and effort, though, caregivers can learn about the legislative process and current child-care issues. *Becoming informed* is the first step in the advocacy process.

One can begin by simply listening to the news on radio or television, and by reading the newspapers. Read journal articles; watch television documentaries related to child care. The publications of professional organizations (such as those listed in appendix H) often have special sections devoted to news updates on legislation affecting children's programs and services. Some groups have advocacy representatives who prepare special bulletins and alert you at critical times to contact your legislators. Local offices of the League of Women Voters are good sources of information; they report current issues, and help you identify your representatives.

Keeping informed is a major responsibility of the child-care advocate. There is a lot to keep up with! *Sharing what you learn* with co-workers, neighbors, and children's parents is the next step for concerned caregivers who want to participate in the advocacy process.

Caregivers can write or call their representatives and encourage others to do so. (Some suggestions for writing legislators are included in appendix I.) Caregivers can also follow through by voting in all elections. Remember candidates' positions on children's issues and vote accordingly.

Caregivers can extend their involvement in advocacy efforts in many ways, deciding how much individual time and effort they can spare. Understand that one person does not have to do everything for every children's program. It is fine to depend on the resources and people already involved in advocacy. Simply discussing with parents the rationales and procedures of your own program, helping them to understand that child care is more than babysitting, is a part of advocacy. More ambitious caregivers may want to organize local advocacy activities and actively lobby on behalf of children. For example, the following illustrates how day-care professionals could respond to a day-care issue—child abuse by day-care workers.

Recently, many child-care professionals have received numerous inquiries about child abuse in day care. Specifically, we have been asked, "How prevalent is child abuse?" and "What can be done to prevent it?" As caregivers, we need to respond to these questions as stated previously, by (1) becoming informed and (2) sharing what we have learned. We have already discussed how caregivers can become informed. We mentioned, for example, reading journals which focus on child care. Two journals, *Child Care Information Exchange* (Hostetler, 1984) and *Young Children* (Koblinsky and Behana, 1984) recently carried excellent articles on child abuse.

For caregivers, sharing information related to child abuse may mean helping to educate parents regarding terms related to sexual abuse, how to recognize signs of sexual molestation, and how they can prepare their children to avoid potential abuse situations.

Many legislators have dealt with the issue of child abuse in day care by creating legislation requiring criminal identification checks. In Illinois, these checks could cost as much as $1.2 million (Hostetler, 1984). However, in several of the incidents reported in the media, the sexual offenders did not have any previous criminal record. Knowing this, Hostetler has suggested that caregivers lobby for funds to be used for adapting available materials on sexual abuse for use with staff, parents, and children, rather than on criminal identification checks.

Regardless of what any individual caregiver chooses to do, remember to value what caregivers as a group do, and help others to understand the nature of group caregiving. This is the beginning of all advocacy efforts.

Burnout

We have outlined, in this text, what is expected of the caregiver. It may seem a lot for any one individual to live up to, and it is. The best caregiver knows that quality care for children does not come easily—it takes time, effort, continual self-reflection and evaluation, and endless interactions with a variety of individuals. Being with a group of toddlers for extended lengths of time can be intense and strenuous. Through no fault of their own, even the most dedicated caregivers wear out. This is a phase that has been characterized by many as "burnout."

Burnout is defined as a "slow and progressive wearing down of body and spirit" (Jorde, 1982); "loss of idealism, energy, and purpose" (Edelwich and

Brodsky, 1980); and the "depletion of personal resourcefulness [and] flexibility" (Seiderman, 1978). The consequences of staff burnout are a deterioration in the quality of care, individual psychological and physical stress, and in many cases the profession's eventual loss of a good caregiver.

Symptoms

A caregiver suffering from burnout experiences emotional and physical exhaustion. The job now seems like too much to cope with. The burned-out caregiver may have frequent headaches; he or she feels strained, overworked, and may complain a lot—or not at all. To the burned-out caregiver, children's behavior problems seem to increase and few days seem to run smoothly. Absenteeism may increase. The caregiver becomes apathetic about child-care issues and her own specific responsibilities. In short, she simply goes through the motions of the daily caregiving routine. Very often, the disillusioned caregiver is filled with self-doubt and blame.

Causes

What brings the ordinarily confident and competent caregiver to this phase in her career? To some extent the degree to which she suffers from burnout depends on her individual stress tolerance level, that is, the ability she has to cope with, and adapt to, situations and events. Her general state of health and diet also have an effect. Stresses outside the job setting (for example, family relationship problems or financial difficulties) also play a role in contributing to burnout.

Sometimes, burnout results when a caregiver "cares too much," and wants to influence and affect children to a greater extent than is humanly possible. Her concerns may be genuine, but her expectations are unrealistic. For example, some caregivers feel they are responsible for teaching parents about child development and effective childrearing. However, some families may not be interested in the caregiver's advice, or may not take time to respond to the caregiver's efforts. Some parents may persist in spanking their child or in being excessively permissive, which the caregiver finds difficult to accept. She feels strongly that the welfare of the child and the family are negatively affected. She expends considerable energy trying to influence the parents. The parents, though, have their own ideas, and it may be that nothing can alter them. This caregiver feels emotionally exhausted since her efforts seem to have had no impact. She may be physically exhausted since time spent with parents was usually in addition to her full-time day-care position. She feels disillusioned and at fault when she doesn't see the results she desired.

More immediate causes of burnout may relate to a caregiver's specific job situation. She may have little or no support or appreciation from her supervisor, co-workers, and/or parents. There may be no mechanisms to include her in decisions being made that affect her position; she is overcome by a feeling of powerlessness. Interpersonal relations among staff members may be full of conflicts and hostilities. The administration may not be responsive to staff members' needs.

Other conditions contributing to staff burnout are those endemic to the caregiving profession. There is considerable day-to-day unpredictability that must be faced when working with young children. The caregiver is often the one in the middle—between administrators, parents, and children—trying to satisfy all their expectations. For many caregivers, when children leave a program, the separation and loss brings repeated sadness that seems hard to bear.

While we write of caregivers as professionals exhibiting professional attitudes and performance, it is frustrating to realize that society does not recognize their professionalism. Being seen by many as "babysitters," as needing few skills and small compensation, angers competent caregivers, who know the importance of what they do. The low pay and low status of caregivers reflects a lack of a national commitment to child care. After some years in the profession, these attitudes, combined with limited paths of advancement within the profession, often affect the caregiver's feelings of self-worth.

Coping

While it may not be possible to prevent burnout, there are some things caregivers can do to counter it before it occurs, and/or after they recognize the problem.

First, as caregivers, we must acknowledge the givens of our chosen profession, understand them, and try to live and work with them. This does not mean that it is hopeless to work toward changing the low status of our profession, or to advocate on behalf of children. Rather, we need to set realistic personal and professional goals, keeping a perspective that focuses on the process, not simply on the results. For a more thorough discussion of coping, we recommend Paula Jorde's excellent book *Avoiding Burnout* (1982).

Lessening stress within the day-care center is possible if one follows the suggestions in this text for managing routines, arranging the physical environment, and coordinating resources. Other strategies for caregivers include:

1. striving for open communication among co-workers and administrators;
2. becoming involved in other operations of the center, including decision making;
3. changing your routine, shift, or the age of the children in your group;
4. arranging with your supervisor for more flexible job responsibilities;
5. attending conferences and inservice workshops.

A lifestyle that includes time for exercise and relaxation also may help relieve the stresses of caregiving. A wholesome diet helps a caregiver stay energetic and healthy to meet job demands. Take advantage of resources that are available to help you. Feel free to be yourself, think well of yourself, and trust yourself. Then it will be easier to be open to growth and change.

Lastly, lest these warnings discourage some potential caregivers, remind yourself of the many satisfactions of our profession—for most of us, the motivation for our own initial interest. Daily, toddlers bring new joys into our lives with their spontaneous laughter and open affection. By entering their world and sharing their discoveries, their expressions of understanding, and their poignant insights into our world, we are simultaneously contributing to our own capacity to view ourselves with humor and appreciation.

References

Ade, W. 1982. Professionalization and its impact for the field of early childhood education. *Young Children* 37 (March), 25–32.

Ade, W., and Weitz-Bell, L. (eds.) 1978. *A guide for child advocacy.* Champaign, IL: Available from the East Central Illinois Association for the Education of Young Children.

Caldwell, B.M. 1983. How can we educate the American public about the child care profession? *Young Children* 38 (March), 11–17.

Children's Defense Fund. 1982. *Child care: A guide for advocates.* Washington, DC: Children's Defense Fund.

Divine-Hawkins, P. 1981. *Family day care in the United States: Executive Summary.* Final Report of the National Day Care Home Study. Washington, DC: Department of Health and Human Services.

Edelwich, J., and Brodsky, A. 1980. *Burnout: Stages of disillusionment in the helping professions.* New York: Human Sciences Press.

Hostetler, L. 1983. Putting our child care skills to work in advocacy. *Child Care Information Exchange* (January/February), 25–29.

Hostetler, L. 1984. 'Regulatory remedies' in the sexual abuse issue: How can child care providers respond? *Child Care Information Exchange* (August), 21–22.

Hyson, M. 1982. Playing with kids all day: Job stress in early childhood education. *Young Children* 37 (January).

Jorde, P. 1982. *Avoiding burnout.* Washington, DC: Acropolis Books.

Koblinsky, S. and Behana, N. 1984. Child sexual abuse: The educator's role in prevention, detection, and intervention. *Young Children,* 39 (September), 3–15.

Seiderman, S. 1978. Combatting staff burnout. *Day Care and Early Education* 5 (Summer), 6–9.

Stevens, J., and King, E. 1976. *Administering Early Childhood Education Programs.* Boston: Little, Brown & Co.

Appendixes

Appendix A
Play Experiences for Toddlers

Activities to Enhance Body Expression and Control

1. Work with small objects of various sizes, shapes, and textures.
2. Draw on grocery bags, newspaper ad sections, cardboard, or wrapping paper on floor or table.
3. Pile lightweight blocks on top of one another to build towers.
4. Climb through, under, over, and between objects. Climb stairs or climber / slide.
5. Use active large-muscle equipment, such as trikes, tunnels, balance beam, and sandbox.
6. Pound with hammer.
7. Pull musical toy.
8. Hop, jump, skip, run, lug, push, and pull.
9. Dress and feed self.
10. Turn pages of book.
11. Paint with fingerpaints, colored water, fruit, vegetables, hair rollers, pine cones, and sponges.
12. Paste with cereal, macaroni, popcorn, beans, paper, wallpaper, cardboard, tissue paper, and fabric.
13. Work puzzles.
14. Blow bubbles with drinking straws in colored water.
15. String beads, buttons, macaroni, foam pieces, thread spools, or pieces of drinking straws.
16. Use everyday mechanical things, such as locks, screw caps, keys, buttons, zippers, snaps, nuts, and bolts.
17. Set actions to music.

Adapted with permission of Resource Report 104 © 1978 Grolier, Interstate.

Activities to Enhance Social and Emotional Development

1. Play pat-a-cake and peek-a-boo.
2. Roll ball to others.
3. Play pretend games.
4. Describe self (hair, features, clothes, shoes, toys).
5. Imitate adult activities (play with broom, dustcloth, and mop, wash table, help cook and bake).
6. Help clean up own mess; be responsible for toys.
7. Pretend play in dress-up clothes.
8. Play "I am a mirror" and "Follow the leader" type games.
9. Play in small groups (three to six).
10. Play with puppets and mirror.

Activities to Enhance Thinking

1. Unwrap and unscrew objects.
2. Combine small objects with larger ones.
3. Match clothes, sizes, cups, spoons, dishes, glasses, toys, and shapes.
4. Identify animals, household objects, and environmental objects.
5. Count plastic silverware or poker chips.
6. Put clothespins inside container.
7. Nest measuring cups inside one another.
8. Use feltboard for grouping and counting.
9. Imitate a cube-block, button, or poker-chip design.
10. Match sounds with sound boxes.
11. Play with faucets, doorknobs, keys, locks, etc. mounted on wood.
12. Roll marbles down an incline.
13. Pour colored water into containers of various sizes.
14. Make a feeling box or bag; guess objects inside without looking.
15. Imitate others' sounds and actions.
16. Play "pretend" games.

Activities to Enhance Language

1. Use words to label objects used or things accomplished.
2. Use relationship words (in, out, over, under, on top, bottom, with, without).
3. Count aloud (fingers, toes, blocks, buttons, thread spools).
4. Demonstrate meanings of words ("loud," "soft").

5. Play singing games.
6. Do finger plays.
7. Read lots of books.
8. Play records.
9. Run simple errands (put towel in basket, book on shelf).
10. Follow directions.
11. Dramatize stories in books through role playing or puppetry.
12. Listen to tape of own voice.
13. Tell stories about self, family, and surroundings.

Appendix B
No-Cost or Low-Cost Materials and Equipment for the Child-Care Center

Suggestions for adding variety and increasing the supply of play materials in the child-care center are outlined below. These materials can stimulate both staff and children to use equipment creatively.

Consider safety first when choosing play materials. This refers to their condition as well as to their appropriateness for toddlers. Refer to the checklist for choosing safe materials in chapter 3.

Materials	Suggested Use
Large boxes, crates, and cartons	Unlimited creative uses, indoors or out; bookcases, toy storage, boats, trains, buses; store or doll-corner furniture; climbing, jumping, steps; TV screen.
Boxes with casters added	Make wagons and push and pull toys.
All sizes of wood and cardboard boxes, cheese boxes	Building, painting; doll furniture, trains; containers to hold materials, such as crayons, beads, etc.
Wooden boards	Building tunnels, bridges; walking or balancing board, slides, jumping, crawling.
Old wheels	For would-be drivers, used with boxes and boards.
Logs—single, stacked, or upright	Climbing, benches, boundary for sand or swing area.

Adapted from *No-Cost or Low-Cost Materials and Equipment for the Child Care Center*, Illinois Department of Children and Family Services.

Materials	Suggested Use
Old auto chassis, rowboat, wagon	For playground.
Barrels (including packing drums, usually available at jewelry and department stores)	Rolling, climbing, crawling and tunneling.
Rubber tires and inflated inner tubes	Swings; crawling, rolling; stepping stones; sand enclosure; trampoline.
Large cartons with paper bags	Make robot or space suits, other costumes.
Milk cartons	Bird nests; straighten and close open end and use for building blocks; planters for seeds or small plants; storage bins for spools, etc. when cut in halves or fourths; housekeeping and store play.
Tin cans—various sizes (smooth edges)	For sand play, nest of cans; building; "telephone"—two tin cans with small hole in bottom, connect with waxed string; bells; sprinklers; pitching games.
Large spools	For stringing; soap-bubble blower; wheels for pull toys.
Small food containers (cans, cereal boxes, milk and cheese cartons, empty plastic bottles, etc.)	For housekeeping and store play, unlimited use in combinations.
Clean dress-up clothes, hats, jewelry, fans, purses, hats, scarves, wallets, "frills," etc.	Housekeeping and dramatic play.
Plastic bottles of different sizes and shapes, funnels, tubes, sponges, strainer	Housekeeping play; water and sand play; pouring; experimentation— unlimited in combination.
Heavy cartons of interesting shapes (five-gallon ice-cream-carton, potato-chip cans)	For making decorative waste- baskets, storage items, drums, furniture.
Attach locks, keys, fasteners, switches, slide bolts, chains, door- knobs, etc. to wood board	Gadget board for manipulative play and cognitive development.

Materials	Suggested Use
Scrap book or basket of different materials (from sandpaper to fur, including crepe, satin, wool, ribbon, cotton, etc.)	For sensory experiences in textures; for language development in describing these items; collages.
Paper bags	Hand puppets, head mask, store play.
Plastic bottles (thoroughly rinsed)	With painted cork legs for making animals, coin banks; cut off handles and top for making a pail, wastebasket; use handle end for funnel; windmills; noise makers. (Since plastic bottles are easily cut and sewed, the possibilities are endless.)
Cigar boxes	Use as above; also, for storage; wagons, with spools; radios.
Egg cartons	Egg-shell garden; compartmentalized jewel boxes; cut for art work.
Cardboard rollers from paper towels or tissue paper	For base of animal bodies and dolls, tree trunks, decorative candles; other art work, megaphone.
Wall paper and upholsterer's sample books, catalogues, magazines; greeting card sample books	For cutting and pasting; decorating doll houses, paper dolls, doll clothes; collages; paper mache; scrap books.
Clothespins	Dolls; fences for doll houses; drum sticks; hanging up easel paintings. Game—dropping or tossing into box or can.
Shirt cardboards	Make good backing for magazine pictures; covers for scrap books and homemade story books; for painting, for drying clay work.
Sponges	Painting—dip sponge into paint and daub on paper; for doll housekeeping; for water play; small pillows and cushions.

Materials	Suggested Use
String	String painting; hand games; collage; fringe.
Drinking staws (cut up), macaroni shapes, cheerios, etc.	Stringing; pasting.
Old socks	Hand puppets; bean bags; doll clothes; bits-of-soap holder.

Picture File

Cut out simple pictures and paste on cardboard or construction paper	Can be used for holidays; story telling; object recognition.
Cover large board or cardboard with piece of flannel salvaged from night gown, robe, etc. Use solid color	Flannel board: may be used by children or teacher for story telling, or as a bulletin board.
Magazine pictures backed with flannel	To be used with flannel board.

Musical and Rhythm Instruments

Shakers	Place pebbles or beans securely inside two paper plates stapled or sewn together or in paper bags. Decorate with crayon, ribbons, crepe paper.
Xylophone	Cut broom or mop sticks into varying lengths; mount on wood slats, covered with felt strips cut from old hat.
Rhythm sticks	Thick, unbreakable sticks about ten or twelve inches long.
Drums and Tomtoms	Inner tubing pulled tightly over both open ends of large cans (fruit juice or coffee cans) or oatmeal boxes. Beat using sticks. The coffee cans with plastic covers may be used just as they are.

Materials	Suggested Use
Wood blocks	Cover one side of a wood block with sand paper; rub two together.
Trumpets/Bugles	Rollers from paper towels or toilet paper. Cover one end with wax paper. Hum or blow into open end.

Appendix C
Guide for Discussion
of Problem Behaviors

Date: _____
Child's Name: _____ Recorder: _____

1. *Description of the behavior that is considered a problem*
   a. Exactly what does the child do that is considered a problem?
   b. How often does the behavior occur?
   c. Under what circumstances does this behavior occur?
      Time of day?
      What is the child doing immediately before and after?
      What are you usually doing?
      What are the other children usually doing?
   d. What do you do when the child behaves this way? (How do you han-
      dle the behavior?)
   e. How long has this behavior been a problem?
   f. Has anyone else recognized the behavior as a problem?
2. *Caregiver's Opinions*
   a. Why do you consider this behavior a problem?
   b. Why do you think the child does it?
   c. What behavior do you feel would be more appropriate than the
      problem behavior? (How do you feel the child should behave?)
3. *Is the behavior normal for a child of this age?*
   a. How old is the child (years and months)?
   b. Is this behavior appropriate for a child this age?
   c. If not, what age is this behavior appropriate for?
4. *Parents' Opinions*
   a. Do the child's parents consider this behavior a problem?
   b. How do parents manage the behavior when it occurs at home?
   c. Why do they think the child does it?
   d. How do parents feel child should behave?

Adapted from S. Kilmer, *A Guide for the Discussion of Problem Behaviors* (Ramsey County
Minnesota Family Day Care Training Project, 1974).

5. *What are the possible reasons for the child behaving this way?*
   a. Environmental
      1) *Physical Surroundings*
         What objects available in the room arrangement and play space might affect how this child behaves?
      2) *Activities and Materials*
         Do you have enough materials for all of the children?
         Do you have enough different activities?
         Do children go outside every day?
         What activities does this child especially like to do?
      3) *Human*
         Caregiver—How does the way you handle the problem behavior affect it?
         Parents—How does the way parents handle the behavior affect it?
         Other children—How does the way other children react affect the behavior?
   b. Do you think the child has any special developmental problems?
      1) Physical?
      2) Intellectual?
      3) Social-psychological?
6. *What are possible ways of handling this behavior?*
   a. What are some specific management techniques that can be used? Can the environment (surroundings or activities) be planned to prevent the problem behavior?
   b. Does this child and/or family need professional diagnosis and assistance?
   c. If so, what are some possible resources?
7. *Action to be taken*

   Exactly what are the next
   steps to be undertaken in   Date
   managing this problem?   Who is responsible?   Completed

Appendix D
Personal History Form

Today's Date _____
Child's Name _____
Child's Birthdate _____

*Personal History**

Dear Parents:

We ask these questions about your child so that we may begin to know him or her and meet his/her needs. We encourage you to talk with your child's caregivers to elaborate on any information you feel will be helpful. Thank you.

1. Is any language other than English spoken in your home?

   Yes _____   No _____

   If yes, what language? _____

2. What sounds or words does your child use?

3. If your child is using the toilet, please describe how you approach him or her at the necessary times; and tell us what words he/she uses when he/she needs to use the toilet.

_____

*A separate form is used to obtain health history.

4. If your child is in diapers, do you use,

    Powder? _____

    Ointment? _____

    Other? _____

5. Does your child have strong likes or dislikes in food?

6. How do you help your child to sleep at naptime? Does he/she have any special "cuddly" or blanket?

7. a. What time does your child usually nap? _____

    b. Approximately how long is your child's nap? _____

8. Does your child have any strong fears, such as fear of animals or storms? (Please describe)

9. What approach to guiding behavior or discipline do you find effective?

10. What is your child's favorite pastime or activity?

11. In a few sentences, please describe your child.

12. Please describe any other information concerning your child that would be helpful for us to know.

Appendix E
Anecdotal Record

Child: _____   Setting/Location: _____
Date: _____   Observer: _____
Time: _____

Observation:
(Use back if necessary)

Interpretation:
(Use back if necessary)

Appendix F
Developmental Record

Child: _____   Setting/Location: _____
Date: _____   Observer: _____
Time: _____

Observation:
(Use back if necessary)

Interpretation:
(Use back if necessary)

Appendix G
Child Assessment Form

Child's Name _____

Child's Age _____

Caregiver _____

Date _____ 19 _____

Child _____

Date _____

DAILY ROUTINE

Area	Comments/Examples	Parents' Comments
1. Eating		
2. Dressing		
3. Brushing teeth/ Washing hands, etc.		

Child _____

Date _____

DAILY ROUTINE

Area	Comments/Examples	Parents' Comments
4. Diapering/ Toileting		
5. Naptime		
6. Arrival/Departure		
7. Other		

Child _____
Date _____

INTEREST INVENTORY

Interest	Comments/Examples	Parents' Comments
1. Water Play		
2. Sand Play		
3. Music		

Child _____

Date _____

INTEREST INVENTORY

Interest	Comments/Examples	Parents' Comments
4. Manipulatives (fine motor)		
5. Housekeeping/ Dramatic		
6. Large muscle play (i.e., bike, climbing)		
7. Crafts (painting, etc.)		

Child _____
Date _____

INTEREST INVENTORY

Interest	Comments/Examples	Parents' Comments
8. Stories		
9. Blocks		
10. Favorite toy or activity		
11. Other		

Child _____

Date _____

ASSESSMENT SUMMARY

Area	Comments
1. Cognitive	

2. Motor

3. Language

Child _____

Date _____

ASSESSMENT SUMMARY

Area	Comments
4. Social	
5. Emotional	
6. Creativity/ Imagination	
7. How does his/her day usually go?	

Appendix H
Educational Organizations, Newsletters, and Journals Associated with Early Childhood[1]

Educational Organizations

AAHPER
American Alliance for Health, Physical Education and Recreation
1201 Sixteenth Street, N.W.
Washington, DC 20036

ACEI
Association for Childhood Education International
11141 Georgia Avenue, 200
Wheaton, MD 20902

ACT
Action for Children's Television
46 Austin Street
Newtonville, MA 02160

American Montessori Society
175 Fifth Avenue
New York, NY 10010

ACYF
Administration for Children, Youth, and Families
Box 1182
Washington, DC 20013

CEC
Council for Exceptional Children
1920 Association Drive
Reston, VA 22091

---

[1]Source: Joanne Hendrick, *Total Learning for the Whole Child*. St. Louis: C.V. Mosby, Co., 1986 edition.

Children's Defense Fund
122 C Street, N.W.
Washington, DC 20001

CWLA
Child Welfare League of America, Inc.
44 East 23rd Street
New York, NY 10010

DCCDCA
Day Care and Child Development Council of America
1401 K Street, N.W.
Washington, DC 20005

ERIC/ECE
Educational Resources Information Center on Early Childhood Education
805 West Pennsylvania Avenue
Urbana, IL 61801

NAEYC
National Association for the Education of Young Children
1834 Connecticut Avenue, N.W.
Washington, DC 20009

National Council for the Prevention of Child Abuse
332 South Michigan Avenue, Suite 1250
Chicago, IL 60604-4357

SACUS
Southern Association for Children Under Six
Box 5403
Brady Station
Little Rock, AR 72215

Newsletters

The Black Child Advocate
Black Child Development Institute
1463 Rhode Island Avenue, N.W.
Washington, DC 20005

Child Health Alert
Box 338
Newton Highlands, MA 02161

ERIC/ECE Newsletter
805 West Pennsylvania Avenue
Urbana, IL 61801

Nurturing News: A Form for Male Early Childhood Educators
187 Laselle Avenue
San Francisco, CA 94114

Report on Preschool Programs
Capitol Publications, Inc.
Suite G-12
2430 Pennsylvania Avenue, N.W.
Washington, DC 20037

Today's Child
Roosevelt, NJ 08555

Journals

American Journal of Orthopsychiatry
American Orthopsychiatric Association
49 Sheridan Avenue
Albany, NY 10010

Beginnings
P.O. Box 2890
Redmond, WA 98073

Child Care Information Exchange
P.O. Box 2890
Redmond, WA 98073

Childhood Education
ACEI
11141 Georgia Avenue, 200
Wheaton, MD 20902

Children Today
Office of Human Development Services
Superintendent of Documents
U.S. Government Printing Office
Washington, DC 20402

Child Development
Society for Research in Child Development
University of Chicago Press
5801 Ellis Avenue
Chicago, IL 60637

Day Care and Early Education
Human Sciences Press
72 Fifth Avenue
New York, NY 10011

Developmental Psychology
American Psychological Association
1200 Seventeenth Street, N.W.
Washington, DC 20036

Dimensions
Southern Association for Children Under Six
P.O. Box 5403
Brady Station
Little Rock, AR 72215

Exceptional Children
Council for Exceptional Children
1920 Association Drive
Reston, VA 22091

Harvard Educational Review
Longfellow Hall
13 Appian Way
Cambridge, MA 02138

Interracial Books for Children Bulletin
1841 Broadway
New York, NY 10023

Journal of Children in Contemporary Society
Hawnton Press
28 East 22 Street
New York, NY 10010

Merrill-Palmer Quarterly of Behavior and Development
Wayne State University Press
Detroit, MI 48202

Nutrition Action
Center for Science in the Public Interest
1755 S Street, N.W.
Washington, DC 20044

Young Children
NAEYC
1834 Connecticut Avenue, N.W.
Washington, DC 20009

Appendix I
Communicating With Your Legislator

Writing Your Legislator

Every legislator is sensitive to grass-roots opinion. He or she keeps in close touch with voters in his/her district. Letters from constituents, which arrive every day in large quantities, are one of the best indications of what these constituents think. The mail gets top priority in legislative offices. Every letter is answered. Don't hesitate to write your legislator, if you have something to say that you think should be called to his attention. Write as soon as possible, so that you may affect the planning aspect of the subject you are writing about.

There is an art to writing a legislator. Here are the fundamental do's:

Do: *Write to the person who can do something about it.* If the issue you are concerned about is one of a federal nature, write your senator or the representative from your district. If it is something of a state nature, write the governor or the senators and representatives representing your area in the state legislature. Finally, if it involves only your city, write the city manager or members of the city council. Don't waste your or your respondent's time, if he or she is not the appropriate person to act on the problem.

Do: *Identify the bill or issue* when you write about a specific legislative action. Try to give the number of the bill or at least its popular title.

Do: *Address your legislator properly.* (The Honorable . . .)

Do: *Write legibly* (handwritten letters are fine if they are readable).

Do: *Be brief and to the point:* discuss only one issue in each letter.

Do: *Use your own words and your own stationery.* If you are writing as the representative of a group, use the organization's stationery.

Do: *Be sure to include your address and sign your name legibly.* If your name could be either masculine or feminine, identify your sex. If you have any family, business, or political connection related to the issue, explain it. It may serve as identification when your point of view is considered.

Adapted from Ade, William and Weitz-Bell, Linda (eds.), *A Guide for Child Advocacy: A Legislative Handbook* (Champaign, IL: East Central Illinois Association for the Education of Young Children, 1978).

Do: *Be courteous and reasonable.*

Do: *Feel free to write if you have a question or problem dealing with the procedures of government departments.* Legislators' offices often may help you cut through red tape, or give you advice that will save you time and effort.

Do: *Write when your legislator does something of which you approve.* This kind of letter is the most appreciated. Legislators hear mostly from constituents who are against something, and this gives them a one-sided picture of their constituency. A note of appreciation will make your legislator remember you favorably the next time you write.

Do: *Know what you are writing about.* Know the facts concerning the issue. Your comments should be meaningful, rather than a vague "for" or "against."

Do: *Write your own views—not someone else's.* A personal letter will carry far more weight than a form letter (which most legislators throw in the wastebasket) or a signature on a petition. Discuss your experiences and your observations, or what the proposed legislation will do to and for you.

Do: *Give your reasons for taking a stand.* The fact that you're bitterly opposed to something is not as effective as telling how it could affect you with specific reasons why. Your legislators are interested in facts on which they can base a decision. Be constructive.

Do: *Share expert knowledge if you have it.* Legislators especially welcome the advice and counsel of people they represent who are experts in the areas that legislation may affect, such as child-welfare issues.

Do: *Write the chairperson or members of a committee holding hearings on legislation in which you are interested.* Remember, however, that you have more influence with the legislators from your district than with any other members of the state legislature or Congress.

There are a number of things you should *not do* in writing your legislator:

Don't: *Write a postcard.*

Don't: *Sign and send a form letter.*

Don't: *Begin on the righteous note of "as a citizen and taxpayer";* a legislator assumes that you are not an alien and knows that we all pay taxes.

Don't: *Apologize for writing and taking his time.* If your letter is short and expresses your opinion, he is glad to give you a hearing.

Don't: *Say "I hope this gets by your secretary."* This only irritates the office staff.

Don't: *Be vague.* Some letters that are received in legislators' offices are couched in such general terms that it leaves the legislator and his staff wondering what in the world the writer had in mind.

Don't: *Just because you disagree politically with your legislator, ignore him and write to one from another district.* Legislative courtesy calls for the delivery by the recipient of such a letter to the congressperson from the district involved.

Don't: *Send a carbon copy to your second senator or representative when you have addressed the letter to the first senator.* Write each one individually; it's the courteous thing to do.

Don't: *Write to the members of the House while the bill is still being considered in the Senate and vice versa.* This bill may be quite changed before it leaves one chamber for another.

Remember: It is the straightforward letter carrying the appeal of earnestness that commands the interest and respect of members of the state legislatures or Congress. Legislators never tire of hearing from constituents who have something to contribute to the welfare of the state or nation. They know we write to make our opinions heard and that they are our representatives.

Sending Telegrams to Your Legislator

Another method as effective as letter writing, although somewhat more expensive for the constituent, is sending a telegram. Most of the **do's** and **don'ts** listed under letter writing also apply in sending telegrams. But remember, it is even more important to be concise and to the point in a telegram.

Telephoning Your Legislator

Telephoning is another more limited method of getting a message across. A secretary receives most calls. The message that is delivered must, by the very nature of a call and the secretary's limited time, be concise. The content will therefore be limited. But calling can be monumentally effective in terms of statistics. Legislators do take note of how many calls they receive on particular subjects.

Visiting Your Legislator

A legislator likes to know when a group of constituents is visiting the legislature. The visitors should let the legislator know well in advance, so possible meeting arrangements can be made.

If the visitor wishes to discuss particular legislation with the legislator, he or she could make an appointment in advance. Know the subject; state your reasons for support or opposition. Specific examples are helpful. Let the legislator present his views fully. Even if you do not agree, leave with a friendly feeling. The interview may affect a later vote on the same measure. Write and thank the legislator for the interview.

Index

About the Authors

Robin Lynn Leavitt, an education specialist with the Psychology Department of the University of Illinois at Urbana-Champaign, was formerly the director of the University of Illinois Infant-Toddler Center. She has been with the University's Developmental Child Care Program for six years training undergraduates to work in day-care programs and collaborating on day-care research. She is currently the director of the Day Care Home Project.

Brenda Krause Eheart is director of the Developmental Child Care Program with the Psychology Department, University of Illinois at Urbana-Champaign. She is a member of the Society for Research in Child Development and the National Association for the Education of Young Children. Dr. Eheart lives in Champaign, Illinois with her husband and two children.